ADDISON-WESLEY'S REVIEW FOR THE AP* COMPUTER SCIENCE EXAM IN JAVA™

AP® EXAM

SUSAN HORWITZ

University of Wisconsin, Madison

PEARSON

Addison
Wesley

Boston San Francisco New York
London Toronto Sydney Tokyo Singapore Madrid
Mexico City Munich Paris Cape Town Hong Kong Montreal

Executive Editor	Susan Hartman Sullivan
Assistant Editor	Elizabeth Paquin
Marketing Manager	Nathan Schultz
Senior Production Supervisor	Jeffrey Holcomb
Project Managment	Techsetters, Inc.
Copyeditor	Cheryl Adam
Proofreader	Techsetters, Inc.
Composition and Art	Techsetters, Inc.
Prepress and Manufacturing	Caroline Fell

Access the latest information about Addison-Wesley titles from our World Wide Web site:
http://www.aw.com/computing

Library of Congress Cataloging-in-Publication Data

Horwitz, Susan (Susan B.), 1955-
 Addison-Wesley's review for the AP computer science exam in Java /
Susan Horwitz.
     p. cm.
Includes index.
 ISBN 0-201-77081-4 (pbk.)
1. Computer science–Examinations, questions, etc. 2. Java (Computer
program language) 3. Advanced placement programs (Education)
I. Title.

 QA76.28.H68 2003
 005.13'3–dc22

                    2003058097

ISBN 0-201-77081-4
2 3 4 5 6 7 8 9 10-PHT-06 05 04 03

CONTENTS

TOPICAL REVIEW CONTENTS

Introduction

This book provides a review of the material that is tested on the College Board's Advanced Placement Computer Science A and AB Examinations. It consists of the following two sections:

The first section provides topical review. This section has nine chapters, covering the main topics that are tested on the AP Computer Science Examinations. Each chapter includes practice multiple-choice questions (and answers) for the material covered in that chapter.

The second section includes some hints on taking the AP Computer Science exams, followed by four complete practice exams (two A exams and two AB exams) with no duplicate questions. Immediately following each exam are the answers to the multiple-choice questions and a set of solutions to the free-response questions (in many cases, multiple solutions are given for the free-response questions, as well as comments pointing out common errors).

AP Computer Science

The Advanced Placement Program offers two computer science exams: Computer Science A and Computer Science AB; the A course is a subset of the AB course. Both courses emphasize computer science concepts (for example, abstraction, algorithms, and data structures) rather than details of language syntax. The AB course involves more in-depth study than the A course; for example, linked lists and trees are included in the AB course, but not in the A course.

Starting in the spring of 2004, both the A and the AB courses will use a subset of the Java language, and all parts of the exams that require reading or writing actual code will use Java.

Complete course descriptions for AP Computer Science A and AB can be obtained from The College Board: (800) 323-7155, or via the AP Computer Science website. To help you access the most up-to-date information, Addison-Wesley maintains a website at:

http://www.aw.com/APjava

with links to course descriptions and other useful information about the AP CS curriculum, case studies, and exams.

The AP Computer Science Examinations

The exams are written by a committee of computer science faculty from universities and high schools, and they are designed to determine how well a student has mastered the key concepts in the A or the AB course. Each exam is three hours long and consists of two sections. Section 1 (one hour and fifteen minutes) includes forty multiple-choice questions. Section 2 (one hour and forty-five minutes) includes four or five free-response questions. The free-response questions usually involve writing Java code to solve specified problems. They may also involve higher-level programming tasks such as the design and analysis of a data structure or algorithm, or identifying errors in faulty code.

Both the multiple-choice and the free-response sections include some questions based on the current year's case study (see Chapter 9).

The multiple-choice and free-response sections of the exams are given equal weight in determining the final exam grade. Final exam grades consist of a number between one and five with the following intended interpretation:

5   Extremely well qualified
4   Well qualified
3   Qualified
2   Possibly qualified
1   No recommendation

Many universities give credit and/or advanced placement for a grade of three or higher.

To compensate for guessing, one-quarter of a point is subtracted for each wrong answer on the multiple-choice questions (whereas omitted questions neither add to nor subtract from the total). Students who get an acceptable score on the free-response questions need to answer about 50 to 60 percent of the multiple-choice questions correctly to get a final grade of three.

Within the free-response section, each question is given equal weight. The free-response questions are graded by a group of college and high-school computer science teachers called readers, under the supervision of a college professor (the chief faculty consultant) who has had extensive previous experience as a reader. Considerable effort is expended to ensure that the grading is consistent and fair. A detailed grading guide is prepared for each question by the chief faculty consultant and is used by all readers of that question. Questionable cases are resolved by the most experienced readers and the chief faculty consultant. Students' names and schools are removed from the questions when they are graded, and the readers cannot see the scores that were given for previous questions. To maximize consistency, each of a student's free-response questions is graded by a different reader, and each reader's work is carefully monitored.

TOPICAL REVIEW

1

Basic Language Features

1.1 Expressions: Types and Operators

Every expression in a Java program has a type. In Java, there are two kinds of types: *primitive types* and *objects*. The AP Computer Science subset includes the following primitive types:

```
int    double    boolean
```

Strings and arrays are two special kinds of objects that are included in the AP CS subset; they are discussed later in this chapter. Other objects are instances of classes, which are discussed in Chapter 2.

Associated with each type is a set of operators that can be applied to expressions with that type. The AP CS subset includes the *arithmetic*, *assignment*, *increment*, *decrement*, *equality*, *relational*, and *logical* operators described below.

Arithmetic Operators	
addition	+
subtraction	–
multiplication	*
division	/
modulus (remainder)	%

All of the arithmetic operators can be applied to expressions of type `int` or `double`. The addition operator can also be used to perform string concatenation: if at least one of its operands is a `String`, then the result is the concatenation of that `String` with the `String` representation of the other operand. For example:

Concatenation Expression	Value of the Expression
`"book" + "worm"`	`"bookworm"`
`"version" + 3`	`"version3"`
`.5 + "baked"`	`".5baked"`

Integer division (when both the numerator and the denominator are integers) results in truncation, not rounding. For example, 2/3 is zero, not one; -2/3 is also zero, not minus one. If you want to round a `double` variable x to the *nearest* integer (instead of truncating it), you can use:

```
(int)(x + .5)
```

when x is positive, and

```
(int)(x - .5)
```

when x is negative.

Casting can be used to convert an `int` to a `double` (or vice versa). For example:

Expression	Value of the Expression
`(int)3.6`	3
`(double)3`	3.0
`(double)2/3`	.667
`(int)2.0/3`	0

Assignment Operators	
plain assignment	=
add-then-assign	+=
subtract-then-assign	-=
multiply-then-assign	*=
divide-then-assign	/=
modulus-then-assign	%=

The types of the left- and right-hand sides of an assignment must be compatible, and the left-hand side must be an *l-value*. (An *l-value* is an expression that has a corresponding memory location. For example, a variable is an *l*-value; the name of a type or a method is not an *l*-value, nor is a literal like 10 or "abc".)

The last five assignment operators listed above are called *compound assignments*; a compound assignment of the form

```
a op= b
```

is equivalent to

```
a = a op b
```

For example:

Compound Assignment	Equivalent Noncompound Assignment
`a += 2`	`a = a + 2`
`a -= b`	`a = a - b`
`a *= 5.5`	`a = a * 5.5`

Assignments are expressions, not statements; the value of an assignment expression is the value of its right-hand side. This means that assignments can be "chained." For example, the following is perfectly legal:

```
int j, k, n;
j = k = n = 0; // all three variables are set to zero
```

Increment and Decrement Operators	
increment	++
decrement	--

The increment operator adds one to its operand; the decrement operator subtracts one from its operand. For example:

Using Inc/Dec Operator	Equivalent Assignment Expression
`a++`	`a += 1`
`a--`	`a -= 1`

Equality, Relational, and Logical Operators	
equal to	==
not equal to	!=
less than	<
less than or equal to	<=
greater than	>
greater than or equal to	>=
logical NOT	!
logical AND	&&
logical OR	||

The equality and relational operators must be applied to expressions with compatible types. The logical operators must be applied to expressions with type `boolean`. An expression involving the equality, relational, or logical operators evaluates to either `true` or `false` (so the type of the whole expression is `boolean`). Expressions involving the logical AND and OR operators are guaranteed to be evaluated from left to right, and evaluation stops as soon as the final value is known. This is called *short-circuit evaluation*. For example, when the expression

```
(5 > 0) || isPrime(54321)
```

is evaluated, the method `isPrime` is not called. The subexpression

```
(5 > 0)
```

is evaluated first, and it evaluates to `true`. Since logical OR applied to `true` and any other expression always evaluates to `true`, there is no need to evaluate the other expression. Similarly, since logical AND applied to `false` and any other expression always evaluates to `false`, the method `isPrime` is not called when the following expression is evaluated:

```
(5 < 0) && isPrime(54321)
```

It will be helpful for students to be familiar with *deMorgan's laws*:

```
! ( x && y ) == !x || !y
! (x || y ) == !x && !y
```

Students should also be familiar with the use of *truth tables*. For example, a truth table can be used to determine which of the following three boolean expressions are equivalent:

```
!(a || b)
(!a) || (!b)
(!a) && (!b)
```

The truth table has one column for each variable and one column for each expression. A row is filled in as follows: First, each variable is given a value (*true* or *false*). Then each expression is evaluated assuming those values for the variables, and the value of the whole expression is filled in. A different combination of values for the variables is used in each row (and the number of rows is the number of possible combinations).

The truth table for the three expressions given above is:

a	b	!(a || b)	(!a) || (!b)	(!a) && (!b)
true	*true*	*false*	*false*	*false*
true	*false*	*false*	*true*	*false*
false	*true*	*false*	*true*	*false*
false	*false*	*true*	*true*	*true*

Two expressions are equivalent if their entries match in every row. So using the truth table given above, we can see that `!(a || b)` and `(!a) && (!b)` are equivalent to each other, but not to `(!a) || (!b)`.

PRACTICE MULTIPLE-CHOICE QUESTIONS

1. The expression

   ```
   !(a && b)
   ```

   is equivalent to which of the following expressions?

   A. `(!a) && (!b)`
   B. `(!a) || (!b)`
   C. `!(a || b)`
   D. `(a || b)`
   E. `(a || b) && (a && b)`

2. Which of the following best describes the circumstances under which the expression

   ```
   !(a && b) && (a || b)
   ```

   evaluates to `true`?

   A. Always
   B. Never
   C. Whenever both a and b are `true`
   D. Whenever neither a nor b is `true`
   E. Whenever exactly one of a and b is `true`

3. Consider the following code segment:

   ```
   int x = 0;
   boolean y = true;

   if (y && (x != 0) && (2/x == 0)) System.out.println("success");
   else System.out.println("failure");
   ```

   Which of the following statements about this code segment is true?

   A. There will be an error when the code is compiled because the first `&&` operator is applied to a non-`boolean` expression.
   B. There will be an error when the code is compiled because a `boolean` variable (`y`) and an `int` variable (`x`) appear in the same `if`-statement condition.
   C. There will be an error when the code is executed because of an attempt to divide by zero.
   D. The code will compile and execute without error; the output will be "success."
   E. The code will compile and execute without error; the output will be "failure."

4. Assume that the following definitions have been made, and that variable x has been initialized.

```
int x;
boolean result;
```

Consider the following three code segments:

Segment I	Segment II	Segment III
`result = (x%2 == 0);`	```if (x%2 == 0) { result = true; } else { result = false; }```	```if (((x * 2) / 2) == x) { result = true; } else { result = false; }```

Which of these code segments sets `result` to `true` if x is even, and to `false` if x is odd?

A. I only

B. II only

C. III only

D. I and II

E. I and III

5. Consider the following code segment:

```
if (y < 0) {
    x = -x;
    y = -y;
}
z = 0;
while (y > 0) {
    z += x;
    y--;
}
```

Assume that x, y, and z are int variables, and that x and y have been initialized. Which of the following best describes what this code segment does?

A. Sets z to be the sum x+y

B. Sets z to be the product x*y

C. Sets z to be the absolute value of x

D. Sets z to be the value of x[y]

E. Sets z to be the value of y[x]

ANSWERS TO MULTIPLE-CHOICE QUESTIONS

1. B
2. E
3. E
4. D
5. B

1.2   Control Statements

The AP Computer Science subset of Java includes the following control statements:

```
if     if-else     while     for     return
```

If and If-Else

The two kinds of `if` statements choose which statement to execute next depending on the value of a boolean expression. Here are the forms of the two statements:

> `if` (*expression*) *statement*

> `if` (*expression*) *statement* `else` *statement*

If you want more than one statement in the `true` or the `false` branch of an `if`, you must enclose the statements in curly braces. In general, it is a good idea to use curly braces and indentation to make the structure of your code clear, especially if you have nested `if` statements. For example:

Good Programming Style

```
if (x < 0) {
    System.out.println( "negative x" );
    x = -x;
    if (y < 0) {
        System.out.println( "negative y, too!" );
        y = -y;
    }
    else {
        System.out.println( "nonnegative y" );
    }
}
```

Bad Programming Style

```
if (x < 0) {
System.out.println( "negative x" );
  x = -x;
if (y < 0)
{ System.out.println( "negative y, too!" );
y = -y; }
else
System.out.println( "nonnegative y" );
}
```

Note that the "good" style shown above is only one of many good possibilities. For example, some programmers prefer to put curly braces on separate lines. They would write the code above like this:

Good Programming Style

```
if (x < 0)
{
    System.out.println( "negative x" );
    x = -x;
    if (y < 0)
    {
        System.out.println( "negative y, too!" );
        y = -y;
    }
    else
    {
        System.out.println( "nonnegative y" );
    }
}
```

While and For

The `while` and `for` statements provide two different kinds of loops or iteration (a way to repeat a list of statements until some condition is satisfied). Here are the forms of the two statements:

`while` (*expression*) *statement*

`for` (*init-expression* ; *test-expression* ; *update-expression*) *statement*

As with the `if` statement, curly braces must be used to include more than one statement in the body of a loop. For example:

```
while (x > 0) {
    sum += x;
    x--;
}
```

A `for-loop`:

`for` (*init-expression* ; *test-expression* ; *update-expression*) *statement*

is equivalent to:

```
init-expression;
while ( test-expression ) {
    statement;
    update-expression;
}
```

In other words, the *init-expression* of a `for-loop` is evaluated only once, before the first iteration of the loop; the loop keeps executing as long as the *test-expression* evaluates to `true`; and the *update-expression* is executed at the end of each iteration of the loop.

Although they can be any expressions, standard practice is to make the *init-expression* be an assignment that initializes a loop-index variable to its initial value, and to make the *update-expression* be an assignment that changes the value of the loop-index variable. The *test-expression* is usually a test to see whether the loop-index variable has reached some upper (or lower) bound. For example:

```
for (k=0; k<10; k++) ...
```

It is important to understand that a loop may execute zero times; this happens for a `while-loop` when its condition is `false` the first time it is evaluated, and for a `for-loop` when its *test-expression* is `false` the first time it is evaluated.

Return

The `return` statement is usually used to return a value from a non-`void` method. For example, the following method reads numbers until a negative number is read, and it returns the sum of the (nonnegative) numbers. (Assume that method `readInt` reads one integer value.)

```
public int sumInts( ) {
    int k, sum = 0;
    k = readInt( );
    while ( k >= 0 ) {
        sum += k;
        k = readInt( );
    }
    return sum;
}
```

A `return` can also be used to return from a method before the end of the method has been reached. For example, here is another version of method `sumInts`. This version uses a `return` statement to exit both the loop and method `sumInts` as soon as a negative number is read.

```
public int sumInts( ) {
    int k, sum = 0;
    while ( true ) {
        k = readInt( );
        if (k < 0) return sum;
        sum += k;
    }
}
```

PRACTICE MULTIPLE-CHOICE QUESTIONS

1. Assume that x is an initialized int variable. The code segment

   ```
   if (x > 5) x *= 2;
   if (x > 10) x = 0;
   ```

   is equivalent to which of the following code segments?

   A. `x = 0;`

   B. `if (x > 5) x = 0;`

   C. `if (x > 5) x *= 2;`

   D. `if (x > 5) x = 0;`
      `else x *= 2;`

   E. `if (x > 5) x *= 2;`
      `else if (x > 10) x = 0;`

2. Consider the following code segment.

   ```
   for (int k=0; k<10; k++) {
       for (int j=0; j<5; j++) System.out.print("*");
   }
   ```

   How many stars are output when this code segment is executed?

   A. 5

   B. 10

   C. 15

   D. 50

   E. 500

3. Consider the following two code segments:

Segment 1

```
int x = 0;
while (y > 0) {
    y--;
    x++;
}
System.out.println("x = " + x);
```

Segment 2

```
for (int x=0; y>0; y--) {
    x++;
}
System.out.println("x = " + x);
```

Assume that `y` is an initialized `int` variable. Under which of the following conditions will the output of the two code segments be different?

A. The output will never be different.

B. The output will always be different.

C. The output will be different if and only if `y` is zero just before the code segment executes.

D. The output will be different if and only if `y` is greater than zero just before the code segment executes.

E. The output will be different if and only if `y` is less than zero just before the code segment executes.

4. The two code segments shown below are both intended to return `true` if variable `A` (an array of `ints`) contains the value `val`, and otherwise to return `false`.

Version 1	Version 2

```
for (int k=0; k<A.length; k++) {
    if (A[k] == val) return true;
}
return false;
```

```
boolean tmp = false;
for (int k=0; k<A.length; k++) {
    if (A[k] == val) tmp = true;
}
return tmp;
```

Which of the following statements about the two versions is true?

A. Only version 1 will work as intended.

B. Only version 2 will work as intended.

C. Both versions will work as intended; version 1 will sometimes be more efficient than version 2.

D. Both versions will work as intended; version 2 will sometimes be more efficient than version 1.

E. Both versions will work as intended; the two versions will always be equally efficient.

5. Consider the following two methods:

```java
public static void printStuff( int x ) {
    int y = 1;
    while (y < x) {
        System.out.print(y + " ");
        y *= 2;
        if (y == x/2) return;
    }
}

public static void mystery( ) {
    int x = 8;
    while (x > 0) {
        printStuff(x);
        x /= 2;
    }
    System.out.println("x=" + x);
}
```

What will be the output when method mystery is called?

A. 1 2 1 1 1 x=0

B. 1 2 1 1 x=0

C. 1 2 2 x=0

D. 1 2 4 x=8

E. 1 2 x=8

ANSWERS TO MULTIPLE-CHOICE QUESTIONS

1. B
2. D
3. A
4. C
5. B

1.3 Strings and Arrays

For the AP Computer Science course, you need to know about two special kinds of objects: *strings* and *arrays*. Computer Science A students only need to know about one-dimensional arrays, whereas AB students also need to know about two-dimensional arrays.

There is an important difference between variables that have primitive types (`int`, `boolean`, or `double`) and variables that are objects. In both cases, each variable has an associated location in the computer memory. However, for a primitive type, the integer, boolean, or double value is stored directly in that location, whereas for objects the location contains a pointer to another chunk of memory where the object is stored. The chunk of memory where the object is stored is allocated using `new`. For a `String`, the allocation usually includes the sequence of characters in the string; if not, an *empty* string (one with no characters) is created. For an array, the allocation includes the size of the array. For example:

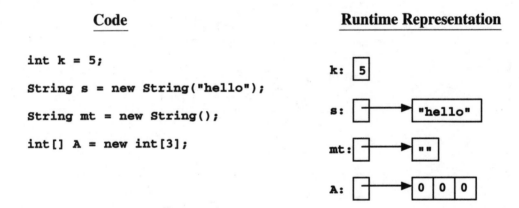

Code	Runtime Representation

```
int k = 5;

String s = new String("hello");

String mt = new String();

int[] A = new int[3];
```

A `String` can also be initialized using a string literal:

```
String s = "hello";
```

and an array can be created and initialized using a sequence of values inside curly braces; for example:

```
int[] A = {10, 20, 30};
```

creates a one-dimensional array of length three, with the values 10, 20, and 30 in `A[0]`, `A[1]`, and `A[2]`, respectively.

The fact that array variables really contain pointers means that it is possible for an assignment to an element of one array to change a value in another array. For example, consider the following code:

```
int[] A = new int[3];
int[] B;
A[0] = 2;
B = A;
B[0] = 5;
System.out.println(A[0]);
```

In this code, A[0] is set to 2 (and there are no other assignments to A[0]). However, the assignment B = A sets variable B to point to the same chunk of memory as variable A. This means that the assignment to B[0] also causes the value of A[0] to change. Therefore, the value printed is 5, not 2. A picture of how each line of code changes the runtime representation is shown below.

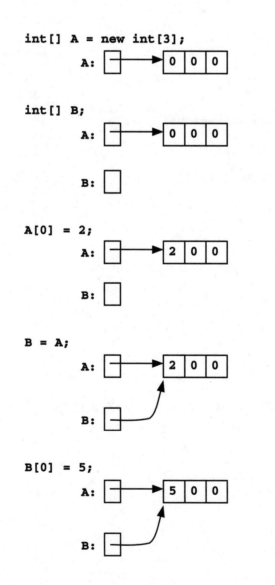

Unlike arrays, `String`s are *immutable*. To understand what that means, remember that a `String` variable S has an associated memory location that contains a pointer to a chunk of memory that in turn contains characters. If you assign to S, you change the pointer to point to a different chunk of memory; you do not change the characters in the original chunk of memory. Here are some pictures to illustrate these ideas:

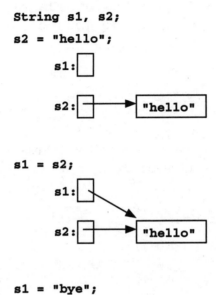

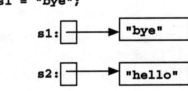

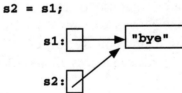

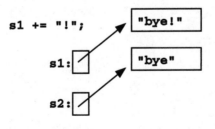

Note that after executing s1 = "bye", the value of variable s2 is still "hello"; assigning to s1 made it point to a new sequence of characters rather than changing the characters in the chunk of memory to which it (and s2) pointed. Even using string concatenation (the + operator) to change s1 simply makes it point to a new chunk of memory that contains the concatenated string; the old chunk of memory (containing "bye") is not affected.

Every array has a field named length that contains the current length of the array. For example, when the following code is executed, the values 3 and 10 will be printed.

```
int[] A = new int[3];
System.out.println(A.length);
A = new int[10];
System.out.println(A.length);
```

Every String has a method named length that returns the current length of the string. For example, when the following code is executed, the values 0, 3, and 1 will be printed.

```
String S = new String();
System.out.println(S.length());
S = "abc";
System.out.println(S.length());
S = new String("?");
System.out.println(S.length());
```

Because Strings and arrays are objects, they inherit the methods defined for the Object class (see Section 3.1.4). For AP Computer Science, you need to know about the equals and toString methods. (AB students also need to know about the hashCode method, which is discussed in Chapter 5.)

The equals method is what you should use to determine whether two Strings are the same. For example, assume that s1 and s2 are String variables. Then the expression s1.equals(s2) (and the expression s2.equals(s1)) will evaluate to true whenever s1 and s2 contain the same sequences of characters.

A comparison of two Strings using the == operator only evaluates to true when the two Strings contain pointers to the same chunk of memory. Here's an example to illustrate the difference between using the equals method and using ==:

Code	Runtime Representation

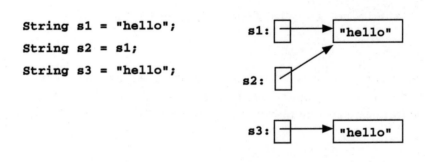

```
String s1 = "hello";
String s2 = s1;
String s3 = "hello";
```

Given these definitions of s1, s2, and s3, here are some expressions that use the equals method and the == operator, and the values of the expressions:

Expression	Value
s1.equals(s2)	true
s1 == s2	true
s1.equals(s3)	true
s1 == s3	false
s2.equals(s3)	true
s2 == s3	false

For objects other than Strings, it is up to the designer of the class to write an equals method that returns true when the two objects are "the same." By default, every object has an equals method that returns true only when the == operator would return true; if the designer of a class doesn't write an equals method, the default one will be used.

It is not possible to define a new equals method for an array, so if A and B are two array variables, A.equals(B) (and B.equals(A)) evaluates to true if and only if A and B point to the same chunk of memory. If you want to test whether two arrays contain the same values, you must write code that looks at the values; you cannot use the array's equals method.

The toString method converts an object to a String. When you use the plus (+) operator to concatenate a String with another object, the other object is converted to a String by calling its toString method. Although every object has a default toString method, those methods usually don't produce a useful string (for example, on my machine, the string returned by the toString method of an array of integers was " [I@7dd0b5aa"). Therefore, if you want to print an array, you will have to write code to do it rather than using the array's toString method.

Two-Dimensional Arrays (AB only)

Here is an example of how to define a two-dimensional array:

```
int[][] A = new int[3][5];
```

When this code is executed, space for a 3-by-5 array (an array with three rows and five columns) is allocated. A common way to initialize an array is to use a for-loop. For example, the following code initializes array A so that each row contains the numbers zero to four.

```
int[][] A = new int[3][5];
int num = 0;
for (int row=0; row<3; row++) {
    for (int col=0; col<5; col++) {
        A[row][col] = num;
        num++;
    }
    num = 0;
}
```

To find out how many rows a two-dimensional array A has, you can use A.length; you can use A[0].length to find out the number of columns. Therefore, instead of using the values "3" and "5" as the upper limits of the two for-loop indexes, we could have used A.length and A[0].length, as shown below.

```
for (int row=0; row<A.length; row++) {
    for (int col=0; col<A[0].length; col++) {
        ...
```

A two-dimensional array can also be initialized using sequences of values inside curly braces. One sequence of values is provided for each row, and each such sequence contains a value for each column in that row. For example, the following code initializes array A to contain the same values as the for-loop given above:

```
int[][] A = {{0,1,2,3,4},{0,1,2,3,4},{0,1,2,3,4}};
```

PRACTICE MULTIPLE-CHOICE QUESTIONS

1. Consider the following code segment (line numbers are included for reference):

```
1.  int[] A = new int[3];
2.  int[] B = new int[10];
3.  B[9] = 30;
4.  A = B;
5.  A[9] = 20;
6.  B[9] = 10;
7.  System.out.println(A[9]);
```

What happens when this code is compiled and executed?

A. Line 5 will cause a compile-time error because of an out-of-bounds array index.

B. Line 5 will cause a runtime error because of an out-of-bounds array index.

C. The code will compile and execute without error. The output will be 10.

D. The code will compile and execute without error. The output will be 20.

E. The code will compile and execute without error. The output will be 30.

2. Which of the following statements is *not* true?

A. Every object has an equals method.

B. If a programmer does not write an equals method for a new class, the default method will return true if and only if all fields of the two instances of the class contain the same values.

C. The equals method for Strings returns true if and only if the two Strings contain the same sequence of characters.

D. The equals method for arrays returns true if and only if the two arrays point to the same chunk of memory.

E. The equals method for Strings will return false if one String is shorter than the other.

3. Consider the following code segment:

```
String s1 = "abc";
String s2 = s1;
String s3 = s2;
```

After this code executes, which of the following expressions would evaluate to `true`?

   I. `s1.equals(s3)`
   II. `s1 == s2`
   III.`s1 == s3`

A. I only

B. II only

C. III only

D. I and II only

E. I, II, and III

4. Consider the following code segment:

```
int[] A = {1, 2, 3};
int[] B = {1, 2, 3};
int[] C = A;
```

After this code executes, which of the following expressions would evaluate to `true`?

   I. `A.equals(B)`
   II. `A == B`
   III.`A == C`

A. I only

B. II only

C. III only

D. I and III only

E. I, II, and III

5. (AB only) Consider the following declaration:

```
int[][] arr = new int[5][6];
```

Which of the following is an object?

A. `arr`
B. `arr[0][0]`
C. `arr[0][0] * 2`
D. `arr.length`
E. `arr[arr.length-1][arr[0].length-1]`

ANSWERS TO MULTIPLE-CHOICE QUESTIONS

1. C
2. B
3. E
4. C
5. A

2

Object-Oriented Features

2.1 Objects, Classes, and Methods

Recall that in Java every variable either has a primitive type (int, double, or boolean for the AP CS subset) or is an *object*. Some objects (e.g., arrays and strings) are built-in to the language. When a programmer designs a program, one important question is what new objects to define, and the answer depends on what the program is designed to do. In general, the new objects will represent the things that the program is designed to manipulate. For example, if a programmer designs a program to be used by a bookstore to keep track of the current inventory, the program will probably include the definition of a new kind of object to represent books.

Each new kind of object is defined by defining a new *class*; for example, we could define the following Book class to represent books.

```java
public class Book {
/*** fields ***/
    private String title;
    private double regularPrice;
    private double salePrice;
    private int numSold;

/*** public methods ***/
    // constructor
    public Book( String theTitle, double price ) {
        title = theTitle;
        regularPrice = price;
        salePrice = price;
        numSold = 0;
    }

    // get the price
    public double getPrice( ) { return regularPrice; }

    // get the sale price
    public double getSalePrice( ) { return salePrice; }

    // sell k copies
    public void sell(int k) { numSold += k; }
```

```
        // lower the sale price
        public void doDiscount( ) {
            salePrice = newPrice(regularPrice, salePrice);
        }

        // determine which book is the most popular
        public static Book mostPopular( Book[] bookList ) {
            // precondition: bookList.length > 0
            // postcondition: returns the book that has
            //                sold the most copies
            int bestNum = bookList[0].numSold;
            int bestIndex = 0;
            for (int j=1; j<bookList.length; j++) {
                if (bookList[j].numSold > bestNum) {
                    bestNum = bookList[j].numSold;
                    bestIndex = j;
                }
            }
            return bookList[bestIndex];
        }

    /*** private methods ***/
        // compute the new sale price
        private static double newPrice(double reg, double sale) {
            if (sale == reg) return (reg * .9);
            if (sale > reg/2.0) return (reg/2.0);
            return(Math.sqrt(reg));
        }
    }
```

Every class has *fields* (also called *instance variables*) and *methods*. The Book class has four fields: title, regularPrice, salePrice, and numSold. It has seven methods: Book, getPrice, getSalePrice, sell, doDiscount, mostPopular, and newPrice.

At runtime, there can be many instances of a class (each one created using new). For our example, there can be many instances of the Book class, each of which represents one book. If a field or method is declared static, then there will be just one copy of that field or method for the whole class; otherwise, every instance of the class will have its own copy of the field or method.

2.1.1 Methods

Each method in a class can be either *static* or *nonstatic*, and can be either *public* or *private*. A method should be nonstatic when it performs a task that is specific to one instance of the class. Most methods are nonstatic. For example, the getPrice and getSalePrice methods of the Book class return the regular and sale prices of one instance of a Book, and the sell method changes the numSold field of one instance of a Book. Therefore, none of these methods is static.

A method should be static when it performs a task that is not specific to one instance of a class. For example, the mostPopular method finds the book in the given array that has sold the most copies. It makes sense for this method to be part of the Book class (since it has to do with books), but since it does not perform a task specific to one book it also makes sense for it to be a static method. Another example of a static method is the sqrt method from the Math class (a class provided as part of the Java language). Math.sqrt (which is used by the Book class's newPrice method) is static since it provides an operation of general use to anyone who wants to perform mathematical calculations; it is not specific to one instance of the Math class (and, in fact, you don't even need to create an instance of the Math class to use the sqrt method).

Now let's consider how to call the static and nonstatic methods of the Book class from code that is not itself part of the Book class. To call a static method of the Book class, you use the name of the class (Book), followed by a dot, followed by the name of the method. To call a nonstatic method of a Book object, you use the name of the object followed by a dot followed by the name of the method. For example, the following code illustrates how to call a static method (mostPopular) of the Book class and a nonstatic method (sell) of a Book object from code that is not part of the Book class. Assume that b is a Book, and B is an array of Books.

```
b = Book.mostPopular( B );   // call Book's "mostPopular" method
b.sell(5);                   // call b's "sell" method
```

Methods that are intended to be used by clients of a class should be public; other methods should be private. For example, the newPrice method performs an operation that is used by the doDiscount method but is not intended to be used by clients of the Book class. Therefore, the newPrice method is a private method. All of the other Book methods are public methods.

Constructors

A *constructor* is a special kind of method. The name of a constructor is the same as the name of the class, and, unlike other methods, a constructor has no return type (not even void). Whenever a new instance of a class is created, a constructor is called to initialize the nonstatic fields of the new object.

The Book class defined above has a constructor that initializes all of its fields. It must be called with two arguments (a String and a double). For example:

```
Book b = new Book("The Cat in the Hat", 5.00);
```

Parameters

Each method has zero or more *parameters*, sometimes referred to as *formal parameters*. The corresponding values used in a call to the method are called *arguments* or *actual parameters*. A method call must include one argument for each of the method's parameters, and the type of each argument must match the type of the corresponding parameter. For example, in the Book class, the newPrice method has two formal parameters, both of type double. The doDiscount method calls newPrice with two arguments: regularPrice and salePrice, both of which are of type double (matching the types of the corresponding parameters).

In Java, all arguments are passed by *value*. This means that what is actually passed is a *copy* of the argument, made when the method is called. Therefore, changes made to the formal parameter by the method have no effect on the argument (since the changes are applied to the copy). For example, suppose we wrote the newPrice method to change its second parameter instead of returning a value:

```
private static void newPrice(double reg, double sale) {
    if (sale == reg) sale = reg * .9;
    else if (sale > reg/2.0) sale = reg/2.0;
    else sale = Math.sqrt(reg);
}
```

And suppose we changed the call in the doDiscount method to:

```
            newPrice(regularPrice, salePrice);
```

In this case, the doDiscount method has no effect on the book's sale price. This is because when method newPrice is called, the value of the argument salePrice is copied into a new location (called sale), and it is the copy that is assigned to. When method newPrice returns, the salePrice field still contains its original value.

However, remember that if an argument is an object, then what is copied is a pointer to the chunk of memory where the object is stored. Changing the formal parameter itself will not affect the corresponding argument, but changing the value *pointed to* by the formal parameter will also change the value pointed to by the argument (since both the argument and the formal parameter point to the same chunk of memory).

Here is some example code to illustrate these ideas:

```
public void changeBook( book b ) {
    b.doDiscount();
    b = null;
}

public void test( ) {
    Book myBook = new Book("Birds", 10.00);
    changeBook( myBook );
    System.out.println( myBook.getSalePrice() );
}
```

When this code executes, the Book constructor initializes both the regular price and the sale price of myBook to $10.00. When method changeBook is called, the value of the argument myBook is copied into a new location (called b). That value is a pointer to the chunk of memory that holds the Book object, including its four fields. When changeBook changes the sale price of b to $9.00 (by calling doDiscount), it changes the value of the salePrice field that is part of that chunk of memory. Since argument myBook is pointing to that same chunk of memory, the value of myBook.salePrice is also changed, and so the value "9.00" is printed after changeBook returns. However, the last statement in changeBook (which sets b to null) only changes the value in the location named b; it has no effect on argument myBook, and so there is no NullPointerException when myBook.getSalePrice is called.

Here are some pictures to illustrate better what happens at runtime:

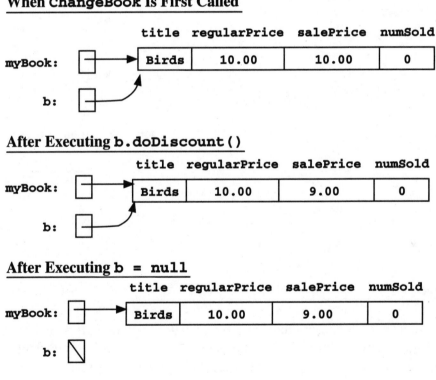

When ChangeBook Is First Called

	title	regularPrice	salePrice	numSold
myBook:	Birds	10.00	10.00	0
b:				

After Executing b.doDiscount()

	title	regularPrice	salePrice	numSold
myBook:	Birds	10.00	9.00	0
b:				

After Executing b = null

	title	regularPrice	salePrice	numSold
myBook:	Birds	10.00	9.00	0
b:				

Since arrays are also objects, the same ideas apply to array parameters, as illustrated below.

Code	**What Happens at Runtime**

```
public void changeArray( int[] B ) {

    B[0] += 5;

    B = null;

}


public void test( ) {

    int[] A = new int[3];

    A[0] = 1;

    changeArray( A );

    System.out.println( A[0] );

}
```

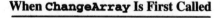

When ChangeArray Is First Called

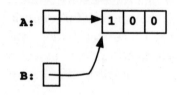

After Executing B[0] += 5

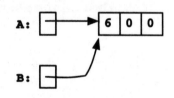

After Executing B = null

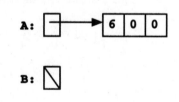

Return Type

Every method (except a constructor) has a *return type*. In general, if a method is designed to perform some action rather than to compute a value, its return type should be void; otherwise, its return type should be the type of the value it is intended to compute. For example, in the Book class, method doDiscount has return type void because its purpose is to modify the book's sale price, not to compute and return a value. In contrast, the purposes of method mostPopular are to determine which book in the given array has sold the most copies and to return that book. Therefore, its return type is Book.

Preconditions and Postconditions

It is a good idea to provide documentation for each method that explains what it does. One good way to do this is to write a precondition and a postcondition for each method. The precondition says what is expected to be true when the method is called, and the postcondition says what will be true when the method returns, assuming that the expectations of the precondition are met. For example, the most Popular method of the Book class (shown again below) has a precondition and a postcondition.

```
public static Book mostPopular( Book[] bookList ) {
    // precondition: bookList.length > 0
    // postcondition: returns the book that has sold
    //                the most copies
    int bestNum = bookList[0].numSold;
    int bestIndex = 0;
    for (int j=1; j<bookList.length; j++ ) {
        if (bookList[j].numSold > bestNum) {
            bestNum = bookList[j].numSold;
            bestIndex = j;
        }
    }
    return bookList[bestIndex];
}
```

It is the responsibility of the programmer who includes calls to mostPopular to make sure that the method's precondition is satisfied on every call; if the array argument has length 0, the programmer cannot expect the method to work as intended. In this case, a runtime error (due to an out-of-bounds array access) would occur. In general, if a method's preconditions are not satisfied, the method might return the wrong value, perform the wrong task, or cause a runtime error.

Recursion

A method that can call itself, either directly or indirectly (for example, by calling another method that calls another method that calls the first method), is called a *recursive* method.

Recursive methods are sometimes much easier to understand than the equivalent nonrecursive code would be. For example, AB students should have seen examples of operations on binary trees that are much more easily implemented using recursive methods than using nonrecursive methods. Both A and AB students should be familiar with the Merge Sort and Quick Sort algorithms, which are also best defined using recursion.

It is important to remember that every recursive method must have a "base case"—a test that can prevent the method from calling itself again; otherwise, a runtime error will occur (for example, a StackOverflowError exception might be thrown). This is usually referred to as an *infinite recursion*, though in fact the limited resources of the computer prevent it from actually being infinite.

Here is an example of a recursive method that does not have a base case:

```
public void printInt( int k ) {
    System.out.print( k + " " );
    printInt( k+1 );
}
```

If `printInt` is originally called like this:

```
printInt( 1 );
```

the output will be:

```
1 2 3 4 5 6 7 8 9 10 11 ...
```

and eventually there will be a runtime error.

Not only must a recursive method include a base case, but it must also "make progress" toward the base case, so that eventually there are no more recursive calls. Here is another version of `printInt`:

```
public void printInt( int k ) {
    if (k < 1) {
        System.out.println( );
    }
    else {
        System.out.print( k + " " );
        printInt( k+1 );
    }
}
```

This version *does* include a base case (the recursive call is not made if k is less than one); however, if `printInt` is originally called with an argument that is greater than or equal to one, the base case is never reached, and there is still an infinite recursion.

Here is a version of `printInt` that never causes an infinite recursion, no matter how it is originally called:

```
public void printInt( int k ) {
// postcondition: Prints the numbers from k to 10,
//                ending with a new line.
    if (k > 10) {
        System.out.println( );
    }
    else {
        System.out.print( k + " " );
        printInt( k+1 );
    }
}
```

It is also important to understand that a recursive method may do some things before the recursive call and may do some more things after the recursive call. The things that are done *after* the recursive call must wait until all of the recursion has finished. For example, consider the two methods shown below (assume that `readInt` reads one integer value).

```java
void echoInput( ) {
    int k;
    k = readInt( );
    if (k != 0) {
        System.out.print( k + " " );
        echoInput( );
    }
}

void reverseInput( ) {
    int k;
    k = readInt( );
    if (k != 0) {
        reverseInput( );
        System.out.print( k + " " );
    }
}
```

The only difference between `echoInput` and `reverseInput` is that `echoInput` prints the value of variable k *before* the recursive call, and `reverseInput` prints the value *after* the recursive call. However, that is a very important difference! Because `reverseInput` waits to print the value of k until after the recursive call has finished, the first value read in to k will be the *last* value printed. For example, if the two methods are each called with the input 1 2 3 4 0, the output of `echoInput` will be 1 2 3 4, and the output of `reverseInput` will be 4 3 2 1.

Overloading

In Java it is possible for a class to have multiple versions of a method with the same name. Such methods are called *overloaded* methods. Two versions of a method must have different *signatures*; that is, they must either have a different number of parameters or at least one parameter must have different types in the two versions of the method (it is *not* good enough for the two versions to have different return types).

Overloading is useful when you want to provide the same operation on different kinds of objects. For example, you might want to define a `max` method for integers and for decimal numbers. You can do this via overloading as follows:

```
public int max( int x, int y ) {
    if (x >= y) return x;
    return y;
}

public double max( double x, double y ) {
    if (x >= y) return x;
    return y;
}
```

In this example, both versions of max have the same number of parameters, but the types of the two parameters differ in each of the versions, so this is legal overloading.

Another reason for using overloaded methods is to provide the same operation with a different number of parameters. For example, you might want to define another version of max that returns the maximum of *three* given integer values rather than two:

```
public int max( int x, int y, int z ) {
    if (x >= y) return max(x, z);
    else return max(y, z);
}
```

The constructors for a class can also be overloaded. When an instance of a class is created using new, the number and types of the arguments are used to determine which constructor is called.

For example, the Book class has a constructor with two parameters (the title and price of the new book). That constructor is called when a new Book is created like this:

```
Book b = new Book( "Happy Days", 22.50);
```

We could define a second constructor, with just one parameter (the title) that initializes the price to some default value. The constructor could be defined like this:

```
public Book( String theTitle ) {
    title = theTitle;
    regularPrice = salePrice = 20.00;
    numSold = 0;
}
```

This new constructor would be called when a Book was created like this:

```
Book b = new Book("Happy Days");
```

Although it is not appropriate for the Book class, a constructor with *no* parameters can also be defined. (This kind of constructor is called the *default* constructor.) If the Book class had a default constructor, it would be called like this:

```
Book b = new Book( );
```

PRACTICE MULTIPLE-CHOICE QUESTIONS

Questions 1 and 2 concern the following (incomplete) Point class.

```
public class Point {
   /*** fields ***/
       private int xCoord;   // the current x coordinate
       private int yCoord;   // the current y coordinate

   /*** methods ***/
    // default constructor: initialize the point to 0,0
      public Point( ) { ... }

    // another constructor: initialize the point to x,y
      public Point(int x, int y) { ... }

    // set the x coordinate to the given value
      public void setX(int x) { ... }

    // set the y coordinate to the given value
      public void setY(int y) { ... }

    // return the x coordinate
      public int getX( ) { ... }

    // return the y coordinate
      public int getY( ) { ... }

    // move the point horizontally d units
      public void moveHorizontal(int d) { ... }

    // move the point vertically d units
      public void moveVertical(int d) { ... }
}
```

1. Assume that `P` is a `Point` variable in a method that is *not* in the `Point` class. Which of the following code segments correctly sets `P` to represent the point (5,5)?

Segment I	Segment II	Segment III
`P = new Point();`	`P = new Point();`	`P = new Point(5,5);`
`P.xCoord = 5;`	`P.setX(5);`	
`P.yCoord = 5;`	`P.setY(5);`	

    A. I only

    B. II only

    C. III only

    D. I and II

    E. II and III

2. Assume that `P` is a `Point` variable that represents the point (x, y) in a method that is *not* in the `Point` class. Which of the following code segments correctly changes `P` to represent the point $(y, x?)$

    A. ```
        P.getX() = P.getY();
        P.getY() = P.getX();
        ```

    B.  ```
        P.setX(P.getY());
        P.setY(P.getX());
        ```

    C. ```
        P.moveHorizontal(P.getY());
        P.moveVertical(P.getX());
        ```

    D.  ```
        int tmp = P.xCoord;
        P.xCoord = P.yCoord;
        P.yCoord = tmp;
        ```

    E. ```
        int tmp = P.getX();
        P.setX(P.getY());
        P.setY(tmp);
        ```
        ```

3. Which of the following best describes the purpose of a method's pre- and postconditions?

    A. They provide information to the programmer about what the method is intended to do.

    B. They provide information to the programmer about how the method is implemented.

    C. They provide information to the compiler that permits it to generate better code.

    D. They provide information to the compiler that makes type checking easier.

    E. They permit the method to be in a different file than the code that calls the method.

4. Consider the following code segment.

```
public void changeParams( int k, int[] A, String s ) {
    k++;
    A[0]++;
    s += "X";
}

public void print( ) {
    int k = 0;
    int[] A = {10, 20};
    String s = "aaa";

    changeParams(k, A, s);
    System.out.println(k + " " + A[0] + " " + s);
}
```

What is output when method `print` is called?

    A. 0 10 aaa

    B. 1 10 aaaX

    C. 0 11 aaa

    D. 1 11 aaaX

    E. 0 11 aaaX

5. Consider the following code segment:

```
public void mystery( int j, int k ) {
    if (j != k) mystery( j+1, k );
}
```

Which of the following best characterizes the conditions under which the call mystery(x, y) leads to an infinite recursion?

A. All conditions
B. No conditions
C. x < y
D. x > y
E. x == y

ANSWERS TO MULTIPLE-CHOICE QUESTIONS

1. E
2. E
3. A
4. C
5. D

2.2 Inheritance

Inheritance is used in a Java program when the objects manipulated by the program form a natural hierarchy using an "*is-a*" relationship. For example, suppose we want to design a program for a bookstore that sells several different kinds of books, including children's books and textbooks. A children's book *is a* book, and so is a textbook. Therefore, we might want to define classes `ChildrensBook` and `Textbook` as *subclasses* of the Book class (and the Book class will then be the *superclass* of both the `ChildrensBook` and `Textbook` classes).

A subclass is defined using the keyword `extends` as follows:

```
public class ChildrensBook extends Book {
   ...
}

public class TextBook extends Book {
   ...
}
```

An advantage of defining classes this way is that subclasses *inherit* all of the fields and methods of their superclasses (except the constructors, which are discussed below). For example, since every book has a title, a regular price, a sale price, and the number of copies sold, there is no need to include those fields in the definitions of the `ChildrensBook` and `TextBook` classes; they will be inherited automatically. Similarly, there is no need to redefine the `sell`, `doDiscount`, `mostPopular`, and `newPrice` methods; every `ChildrensBook` and every `TextBook` will have those methods.

Note that the relationship between a book and a title is a "*has-a*" relationship (a book *has a* title), not an "*is-a*" relationship. That is why `title` is a field, not a subclass, of a Book.

Usually, a subclass will define some new fields and/or methods that are not defined by its superclass. For example, a `ChildrensBook` might include the age of the children for whom it is intended, and a `TextBook` might include the name of the course for which it is required:

```
public class ChildrensBook extends Book {
   /*** new field ***/
     private int childsAge;

   /*** new method ***/
     public int getAge() { return childsAge; }
}

public class TextBook extends Book {
   /*** new field ***/
     private String requiredBy;

   /*** new method ***/
     public String getRequiredBy( ) { return requiredBy; }
}
```

Constructors

As mentioned above, the constructors of a superclass are *not* inherited by its subclasses. However, a subclass's constructors always call a superclass constructor, either explicitly or implicitly. A superclass constructor is called explicitly using super. For example, we could define a constructor for the ChildrensBook class to include an explicit call to the Book constructor like this:

```
public ChildrensBook(String theTitle, double price, int age) {
    super(theTitle, price);
    childsAge = age;
}
```

When this ChildrensBook constructor is called, it first calls the Book constructor to initialize the title, regularPrice, salePrice, and numSold fields; it then initializes the childsAge field itself.

Note that if an explicit call to the superclass's constructor is included, it must be the *first* statement in the subclass's constructor.

If a subclass's constructor does not include an explicit call to one of its superclass's constructors, then there will be an *implicit* call to the superclass's default constructor (i.e., the compiler will add a call). If the superclass does not have a default constructor, this implicit call will cause a compile-time error. For example, if we failed to include an explicit call to super in the ChildrensBook or TextBook constructors, we would get a compile-time error since the Book class has no default constructor.

Using a Subclass Instead of a Superclass

Another advantage of using inheritance is that you can use a subclass object anywhere that a superclass object is expected. For example, because every textbook *is a* book, any method that has a parameter of type Book can be called with an argument of type TextBook; you do not have to write two versions of the method, one for Book parameters and the other for TextBook parameters. For example, the following method computes the difference between a book's regular price and its sale price:

```
public double priceDifference( Book b ) {
    return(b.getPrice() - b.getSalePrice());
}
```

The method will work just fine if it is called with either a Book or a TextBook:

```
Book b = ...
TextBook tb = ...
double d1 = priceDifference(b);  // call with a Book argument
double d2 = priceDifference(tb); // call with a TextBook argument
```

Similarly, it is fine to assign from a TextBook to a Book, because a Book is expected on the right-hand side of the =, and a TextBook *is a* Book:

```
TextBook tb = ...
Book b = tb;              // assign from a TextBook to a Book
```

Although a subclass object can be used anywhere a superclass object is expected, the reverse is not true: in general, you cannot use a superclass object where a subclass object is expected. For example, you cannot call a method that has a TextBook parameter with a Book argument, and you cannot assign from a Book to a TextBook. To illustrate this, assume that the following method has been defined in the TextBook class:

```
public static boolean sameClass( TextBook tb1, TextBook tb2 ) {
    return ((tb1.requiredBy).equals(tb2.requiredBy));
}
```

The following code would cause two compile-time errors, as noted in the comments:

```
Book b = ...
TextBook tb = b; // compile-time error!
                 // can't assign from a Book to a TextBook
if (TextBook.sameClass( b, tb )) ... // compile-time error!
                                     // can't use a Book argument
                                     // when the corresponding
                                     // parameter is a TextBook
```

If you know that a particular Book variable is actually pointing to a TextBook object, then you can use a *class cast* to tell the compiler that it is OK to use that variable where a TextBook is expected. For example:

```
Book b = new TextBook(...);     // b points to a TextBook object
TextBook tb;

tb = (TextBook)b;                                  // no compile-time
                                                   // error
if (TextBook.sameClass( (TextBook)b, tb )) ... // no compile-time
                                                   // error
```

Although the use of a class cast prevents a compile-time error, a runtime check is still performed to make sure that the Book variable really is pointing to a TextBook object. If not, an exception is thrown. For example:

```
Book b = new Book(...);  // b points to a Book object
TextBook tb;

tb = (TextBook)b; // runtime error!
                  // b points to a Book, not a TextBook
if (TextBook.sameClass( (TextBook)b, tb )) ... // runtime error!
                                               // b points to a Book,
                                               // not a TextBook
```

Class casts are often required when using the standard Java classes that implement collections of objects (see Chapter 3). For example, the ArrayList class can be used to represent a list of any kind of object; therefore, the return type of its get method is Object.

When you write code to get an object of a particular type from an `ArrayList`, you will need to use a cast. For example, here is code that creates an `ArrayList` of `Book`s, then prints their prices:

```
// create 3 books and an empty ArrayList
   Book b1 = new Book("Half Magic", 10.95);
   Book b2 = new Book("Magic by the Lake", 15.95);
   Book b2 = new Book("Knights Castle", 12.50);
   ArrayList list = new ArrayList( );

// add the books to the list
   list.add(b1);
   list.add(b2);
   list.add(b3);

// get the books from the list (using casting) and print their prices
   for (int j=0; j<list.size(); j++) {
       Book oneBook = (Book)(list.get(j))      // cast needed here!
       System.out.println(oneBook.getPrice());
   }
```

Overloading and Overriding Methods

Just as a class can define *overloaded* methods (methods with the same name but different signatures), a subclass can overload a method of its superclass by defining a method with the same name but a different signature. For example, the designer of the `ChildrensBook` class might want a second version of the `mostPopular` method that finds the most popular book for children of a particular age:

```
public static Book mostPopular( Book[] bookList, int age ) {
    // precondition: bookList.length > 0
    // postcondition: returns the book intended for children of
    //                the given age that has sold the most copies

       ...
}
```

In addition to overloading methods defined by its superclass, a subclass can also *override* a superclass method; that is, it can define a new version of the method specialized to work on subclass objects. A superclass method is overridden when the subclass defines a method with exactly the same name, the same number of parameters, and the same types of parameters as the superclass.

For example, a special formula might be used to compute the sale price of children's books (different from the formula used for other kinds of books). In this case, the `ChildrensBook` class might override the `Book` class's definition of the `doDiscount` method as follows:

```
// lower the sale price for a childrens book (by 20%)
public void doDiscount( ) {
    salePrice = salePrice * .8;
}
```

As discussed above, a variable of type Book may actually point to a Book object, a TextBook object, or a ChildrensBook object. The type of the object actually pointed to (not the declared type of the variable) is what determines which version of an overridden method is called (this is known as *dynamic dispatch*). For example:

```
Book b = new Book(...);
Book tb = new TextBook(...);
Book cb = new ChildrensBook(...);

b.doDiscount();   // b points to a Book object, so the Book
                  // class's doDiscount method is called
tb.doDiscount();  // tb points to a TextBook object;
                  // the doDiscount method was not overridden
                  // in the TextBook class, so the Book class's
                  // doDiscount method is called
cb.doDiscount();  // cb points to a ChildrensBook object;
                  // the doDiscount method was overridden in the
                  // ChildrensBook class, so the ChildrensBook
                  // class's doDiscount method is called
```

In this example, variables b, tb, and cb are all declared to be of type Book. However, tb is initialized to point to a TextBook, and cb is initialized to point to a ChildrensBook. The calls b.doDiscount() and tb.doDiscount() cause the Book class's doDiscount method to be called (because b points to a Book, and because tb points to a TextBook and the TextBook class does not override the doDiscount method). The call cb.doDiscount() causes the ChildrensBook class's doDiscount method to be called (because cb points to a ChildrensBook, and that class *does* override the doDiscount method).

Abstract Methods and Classes

Suppose you want to define a class hierarchy in which some method needs to be provided by all subclasses, but there is no reasonable default version (i.e., it is not possible to define a version of the method in the superclass that makes sense for the subclasses). For example, you might define a Shape class with three subclasses: Circle, Square, and Rectangle. A Circle will have fields that specify the coordinates of its center and its radius. A Square will have fields that specify the coordinates of its upper-left corner and the length of one side. A Rectangle will have fields that specify the coordinates of its upper-left corner, its height, and its width.

It will be useful to have a Draw method for all Shapes; however, there is no reasonable Draw method that will work for a Circle, a Square, and a Rectangle. This is a time to use an *abstract method*: a method that is *declared* in a class but defined only in a subclass. (For our example, the Draw method will be the abstract method; it will be declared in the Shape class, and it will be defined in each of the three subclasses: Circle, Square, and Rectangle.)

Here's the syntax:

```
public abstract class Shape {
    abstract public void Draw();  // no body, just the method header
}

public class Circle extends Shape {
    public void Draw() {
       // code for Circle's Draw method goes here
    }
}

public class Square extends Shape {
    public void Draw() {
       // code for Square's Draw method goes here
    }
}

public class Rectangle extends Shape {
    public void Draw() {
        // code for Rectangle's Draw method goes here
    }
}
```

Note that if a class includes an abstract method, the class *must* be declared abstract, too (otherwise you get a compile-time error). Also, an abstract class cannot be instantiated (you cannot create an instance of the class itself, only of one of its subclasses). For example:

```
Shape s;             // OK -- just a pointer to a Shape,
                     //        no attempt to create a Shape object
s = new Circle();  // OK -- Circle is not an abstract class
s = new Shape();   // Error!  Can't instantiate an abstract class
```

Interfaces

Some objects have more than one "is-a" relationship. For example, consider designing classes to represent some of the people associated with a university. One way to think of the hierarchical relationship among those people is as shown below:

```
        Person
     /          \
Student        Teacher
   |
  TA
```

This diagram says that a TA (a teaching assistant) is a student, a student is a person, and a teacher is also a person. However, although a TA is certainly a student, in some ways, a TA is also a teacher (e.g., a TA teaches a class and gets paid). Java does not allow you to make the TA class a subclass of both the Student class and the Teacher class. One solution to this problem is to make TA a subclass of the Student class and to use an *interface* to define what TAs and teachers have in common.

An interface is similar to a class, but it can only contain:

- public, static, final fields (i.e., constants)
- public, abstract methods (i.e., just method headers, no bodies)

Here's an example:

```
public interface Employee {
    void raiseSalary( double d );
    double getSalary();
}
```

Note that both methods are implicitly public and abstract (those keywords can be provided, but are not necessary).

A class can *implement* one or more interfaces (in addition to extending one class). It must provide bodies for all of the methods declared in the interface, or else it must be abstract. For example:

```
public class TA implements Employee extends Student {
    public void raiseSalary( double d ) {
        // actual code here
    }
    public double getSalary() {
        // actual code here
    }
}
```

Many classes can implement the same interface (e.g., both the TA class and the Teacher class can implement the Employee interface). Interfaces provide a way to group similar objects. For example, you could write a method with a parameter of type Employee, and then call that method with either a TA or a Teacher object. If you hadn't used the Employee interface (e.g., if you simply wrote raiseSalary and getSalary methods for the TA and Teacher classes), writing such a method would be very clumsy.

PRACTICE MULTIPLE-CHOICE QUESTIONS

1. Consider writing a program to be used by a restaurant to keep track of the items on the menu, which include appetizers, main dishes, and desserts. The restaurant wants to keep track, for every menu item, of the ingredients needed to prepare that item. Some operations will be implemented that apply to all menu items, and there will also be some specialized operations for each of the three different kinds of menu items.

    Which of the following is the best design?

    A. Define a superclass `MenuItem` with three subclasses: `Appetizer`, `MainDish`, and `Dessert`, and with an `Ingredients` field.

    B. Define a superclass `MenuItem` with four subclasses: `Appetizer`, `MainDish`, `Dessert`, and `Ingredients`.

    C. Define three unrelated classes: `Appetizer`, `MainDish`, and `Dessert`, each of which has an `Ingredients` field.

    D. Define four classes: `Appetizer`, `MainDish`, `Dessert`, and `Ingredients`. Make `Ingredients` a subclass of `Dessert`, make `Dessert` a subclass of `MainDish`, and make `MainDish` a subclass of `Appetizer`.

    E. Define one class `MenuItem` with four fields: `Appetizer`, `MainDish`, `Dessert`, and `Ingredients`.

Questions 2 and 3 refer to the following (incomplete) class definitions.

```
public class Person {
  public Person() { ... }
  public void print() { System.out.println("person"); }
  public static void printAll( Person[] list ) {
     for (int k=0; k<list.length; k++) list[k].print();
  }
}

public class Student extends Person {
  public void print() { System.out.println("student"); }
}
```

2. Consider the following code:

```
ArrayList L = new ArrayList();
Student s;
Person p = new Person();
L.add(p);
statement
```

   Which of the following can be used to replace the placeholder *statement* so that the code will cause neither a compile-time nor a runtime error?

   A. `p = (Student)(L.get(0));`

   B. `p = (Person)(L.get(0));`

   C. `s = L.get(0);`

   D. `s = (Person)(L.get(0));`

   E. `s = (Student)(L.get(0));`

3. Assume that method `printAll` is called with an array of length 5, and that none of the five elements of the array is null. Which of the following statements best describes what will happen, and why?

   A. The word `person` will be printed five times since the type of the array parameter is `Person`.

   B. The word `person` will be printed five times since `printAll` is a method of the `Person` class.

   C. The word `student` will be printed five times since the `print` method was overridden by the `Student` class.

   D. For each of the five objects in the array, either the word `person` or the word `student` will be printed, depending on the type of the object.

   E. If the array actually contains objects of type `Person`, then the word `person` will be printed five times; otherwise, a runtime error will occur.

4. Consider the following (incomplete) class definitions:

```
public abstract class Shape {
    public Shape() { ... }

    public abstract void print();
}

public class Square extends Shape {
    public Square() { ... }

    public void print() {
        System.out.println("square");
    }
}
```

Which of the following statements does *not* cause a compile-time error?

   I. `Shape s = new Square();`
  II. `Shape s = new Shape();`
 III. `Square s = new Shape();`

A. I only

B. II only

C. III only

D. I and II only

E. II and III only

5. Consider the following interface and class definitions:

```
public interface Employee {
    void raiseSalary();
}

public interface Musician {
    void Play();
}

public class Test implements Employee, Musician {
    public void raiseSalary() {
        System.out.println("raising");
    }

    public void Play() {
        System.out.println("playing");
    }
}
```

Which of the following statements about these definitions is true?

A. The code will not compile because class `Test` tries to implement two interfaces at once.

B. The code will not compile because class `Test` only implements interfaces; it does not extend any class.

C. The code will not compile because class `Test` only implements the methods defined in the `Employee` and `Musician` classes; it does not define any new methods.

D. The code will compile; however, if class `Test` did not include a definition of the `Play` method, the code would not compile.

E. The code will compile; furthermore, even if class `Test` did not include a definition of the `Play` method, the code would compile.

ANSWERS TO MULTIPLE-CHOICE QUESTIONS

1. A
2. B
3. D
4. A
5. D

3

AP Computer Science Standard Interfaces and Classes

The AP exams will make use of a set of standard interfaces and classes defined in the packages `ap.java.lang`, `ap.java.util`, and `ap`. The interfaces and classes in `ap.java.lang` and `ap.java.util` are also defined in the Java packages `java.lang` and `java.util`; however, the Java versions generally include more methods than the AP versions. The interfaces and classes in the `ap` package have no analog in Java; they are defined specially for use in the AP courses and on the AP exams.

The standard AP interfaces and classes are defined and discussed below. A "quick reference" guide that summarizes them is given at the very end of this chapter. A similar guide (but possibly containing just the names of the classes, interfaces, and methods with no explanations) will be provided as part of the AP CS exams.

3.1 Interface and Classes from the *ap.java.lang* Package

3.1.1 The *ap.java.lang.Comparable* Interface

This interface is used for objects that have a "natural ordering"; that is, objects for which it makes sense to say that one is "less than" or "comes before" another. For example, the `String`, `Integer`, and `Double` classes all implement the `Comparable` interface.

The AP CS Java subset includes only one `Comparable` method:

Method	Explanation
`int compareTo(Object other)`	Returns a negative integer, zero, or a positive integer depending on whether this `Object` is less than, equal to, or greater than `other`.

3.1.2 The *ap.java.lang.Double* and *ap.java.lang.Integer* classes

Both the `Double` class and the `Integer` class implement the `ap.java.lang.Comparable` interface (described above in Section 3.1.1). Each `Double` represents a double value, and each `Integer` represents an int value. The AP CS Java subset includes the following `Double` and `Integer` methods:

Method	Explanation
`Double(double d)`	Constructs a new `Double` that represents d.
`double doubleValue()`	Returns the `double` represented by this `Double`.
`Integer(int k)`	Constructs a new `Integer` that represents k.
`int intValue()`	Returns the `int` represented by this `Integer`.
`int compareTo(Object other)`	Returns a negative integer, zero, or a positive integer depending on whether this `Double`/`Integer`'s value is less than, equal to, or greater than `other`'s value.
`boolean equals(Object other)`	Returns `true` if `other` is the same kind of `Object` (`Double` or `Integer`) as this one and has the same value; otherwise, returns `false`.

The `Double` and `Integer` classes are provided so that you can use objects that represent `ints` and `doubles`. For example, you might want to create a list of integers using the `ArrayList` class (described below in Section 3.2.5), but an `ArrayList` is a list of `Objects`, and integers are not `Objects`. The way to get around this is to "package up" the integers you want in the list using `Integers`. When you need the (plain) integer values, you can get them back using the `intValue` method.

For example, here is code that creates a list of the integers from 1 to 10, then prints them in order.

```
ArrayList list = new ArrayList( );
for (int k=1; k<=10; k++) {
    list.add(new Integer(k));
}
for (int k=0; k<list.size(); k++) {
    Integer tmp = (Integer)list.get(k);
    System.out.println(tmp.intValue( ));
}
```

Note that the `ArrayList`'s `get` method returns an `Object`, not an `Integer`. Because of this, if the second `for-loop` in the above code were written as follows:

```
for (int k=0; k<list.size(); k++) {
    Integer tmp = list.get(k);
    System.out.println(tmp.intValue( ));
}
```

we would get a compile-time error because the type of the right-hand side of the assignment—`Object`—is not compatible with the type of the left-hand side—`Integer`. However, since we know that the result of calling `get` is in fact an `Integer`, we can use casting to change the type of the right-hand side from `Object` to `Integer`, thus preventing the compile-time error.

3.1.3 The *ap.java.lang.Math* class

The `Math` class provides a number of standard mathematical functions. The AP CS Java subset includes the following `Math` methods:

Method	Explanation
`static int abs(int x)`	Returns the absolute value of `int x`.
`static double abs(double x)`	Returns the absolute value of `double x`.
`static double pow(double base, double exponent)`	Returns the value of base raised to the power of `exponent`.
`static double sqrt(double x)`	Returns the square root of `x`.

Note that all of the `Math` methods are *static*. This means that when you want to use a `Math` method, you use the class name followed by a dot followed by the method name, instead of using the name of a `Math` object followed by a dot followed by the method name. For example, the code fragment below includes a use of the abs (absolute value) method of the `Math` class:

```
double d = -2.0;
double posd = Math.abs(d);  // posd is 2.0
```

3.1.4 The *ap.java.lang.Object* class

As discussed in Chapter 1, objects are the basic building blocks of object-oriented programs. The AP CS Java subset includes the following `Object` methods:

Method	Explanation
`boolean equals(Object other)`	Returns `true` if this `Object` is the same as `other`; otherwise, returns `false`. (Note that the default version returns `true` if and only if the `==` operator returns `true`; i.e., if and only if this `Object` points to the same chunk of memory as `other`.)
`int hashCode()` (AB only)	Returns a hashcode value for this `Object`. (See Chapter 5 for more information about the `hashCode` method.)
`String toString()`	Returns a string representation of this `Object`.

Remember that every class is a subclass of `Object`, so every class inherits the `equals`, `toString`, and `hashCode` methods of the `Object` class. However, it is often a good idea to override these methods when you define a new class so that you get more suitable versions.

For example, consider the following (partial) definition of the `Person` class:

```java
public class Person {
   /*** fields ***/
      private String name;
      private String address;

   /*** public methods ***/
      // constructor
      public Person(String initName, String initAddress) {
          name = initName;
          address = initAddress;
      }
      // other methods
      ...
}
```

Now consider the following code fragment:

```java
Person p1 = new Person("Chris Smith", "123 Willow St");
Person p2 = new Person("Chris Smith", "123 Willow St");
if (p1.equals(p2)) System.out.println("equal");
else System.out.println("not equal");
```

If the `Person` class does not override the default `equals` method (inherited from the `Object` class), `"not equal"` will be printed, because `p1` and `p2` point to different chunks of storage. If we want two `People` objects with the same name and the same address to be considered equal, we must include a new definition of the `equals` method in the `Person` class:

```
public boolean equals(Person p) {
    return (name.equals(p.name) && address.equals(p.address));
}
```

3.1.5 The *ap.java.lang.String* class

The `String` class implements the `ap.java.lang.Comparable` interface (described in Section 3.1.1). An instance of the `String` class represents a sequence of zero or more characters. The AP CS Java subset includes the following `String` methods:

Method	Explanation
`int compareTo(Object other)`	If `other` is not a `String`, throws an exception. Otherwise, returns a negative number if this string comes before `other` in lexicographic order; returns a positive number if this string comes after `other` in lexicographic order; returns zero if the two strings are the same.
`boolean equals(Object other)`	Returns `true` if `other` is a string with the same sequence of characters as this one; otherwise, returns `false`.
`int indexOf(String s)`	Returns the position of the first occurrence of `s` in this string, or -1 if `s` does not occur in this string.
`int length()`	Returns the number of characters in this string.
`String substring(int from, int to)`	Returns the substring that starts with the character in position `from` and ends with the character in position `to`-1 (counting from zero).
`String substring(int from)`	Returns the substring that starts with the character in position `from` (counting from zero) and ends with the last character in the string.

PRACTICE MULTIPLE-CHOICE QUESTIONS

1. Consider the following code segment:

```
String S = "razzle-dazzle";
int k;
k = S.indexOf("z");
while (k != -1) {
    S = S.substring(0, k) + "p" + S.substring(k+1);
    k = S.indexOf("z");
}
System.out.println(S);
```

What is output when this code segment is executed?

A. `rapple-dapple`

B. `rapzle-dazzle`

C. `razzle-dazple`

D. `razzle-dazzle`

E. `ra`

2. Assume that variable A is an array of `Strings` and that variable S is a `String`. Consider the following code segment:

```
for (int k=0; k<A.length; k++) {
    if (A[k].compareTo(S) < 0) return false;
}
return true;
```

When does this code segment return `true`?

A. When all of the strings in A come before S in lexicographical order

B. When no string in A comes before S in lexicographical order

C. When no string in A comes after S in lexicographical order

D. When some string in A comes before S in lexicographical order

E. When some string in A comes after S in lexicographical order

Questions 3 and 4 concern the following code segment (line numbers are included for use in question 4). Assume that variable S is a `String`.

```
1. int k = 0;
2. for (int j = S.length()-1; j>=0; j--) {
3.     if (!  (S.substring(k,k+1).equals(S.substring(j,j+1))))
           return false;
4.     k++;
5. }
6. return true;
```

3. Which of the following best describes what this code segment does?

    A. Always returns `true`

    B. Always returns `false`

    C. Determines whether S is the same forwards and backwards

    D. Determines whether S contains any duplicate characters

    E. Determines whether the characters in S are in sorted order

4. Consider changing the code segment to make it more efficient. Which of the following changes would accomplish that without changing what the method does?

    A. Change line 2 to:

```
for (int j = S.length()-1; j>=S.length()/2; j--)
```

    B. Change line 2 to:

```
for (int j=0; j<=S.length(); j++)
```

    C. Change line 3 to:

```
if (S.substring(k, k+1).equals(S.substring(j, j+1)))
    return true;
```

    and change line 6 to:

```
return false;
```

    D. Change line 3 to:

```
if (!(S.substring(k, k+1).equals(S.substring(j, j+1))) ||
    !(S.substring(k+1, k+2).equals(S.substring(j-1, j))))
    return false;
```

    E. Change line 3 to:

```
if (!(S.substring(k, k+1).equals(S.substring(j, j+1))) ||
    (j < k)) return false;
```

5. Consider the following methods:

```
public static void trySwap(int k, Integer K) {
    int tmp = K.intValue( );
    K = new Integer(k);
    k = tmp;
}

public static void test( ) {
    int n = 5;
    Integer N = new Integer(10);
    trySwap(n, N);
    System.out.println(n + " " + N);
}
```

What is output when method `test` executes?

A.   10 5

B.   5 5

C.   5 10

D.   10 10

E.   Nothing is output; a `NullPointerException` is thrown when `trySwap` is called.

ANSWERS TO MULTIPLE-CHOICE QUESTIONS

1. A
2. B
3. C
4. A
5. C

3.2 Interfaces and Classes from the *ap.java.util* Package

3.2.1 The *ap.java.util.Iterator* and *ap.java.util.ListIterator* Interfaces (AB only)

These two interfaces are used to provide a way to iterate through the objects in some collection of objects, one at a time. They also allow an object to be removed from the collection after it has been "visited" during an iteration.

Every class that implements the `Set` interface (e.g., the `HashSet` and `TreeSet` classes) has a method called `iterator` that returns an `Iterator`, and every class that implements the `List` interface (e.g., the `ArrayList` and `LinkedList` classes) includes both an `iterator` method (that returns an `Iterator`) and a `listIterator` method (that returns a `ListIterator`).

The basic iteration methods (provided by both interfaces) are:

Method	Explanation
`boolean hasNext()`	Returns `true` if the collection has more elements; otherwise, returns `false`.
`Object next()`	Returns the next element in the collection.
`void remove()`	Removes the last element returned by the iterator from the collection.

Here is some code that illustrates how to use an iterator. It first creates a `HashSet` containing the values from one to ten, then uses an iterator to print all of the values. Note that the values may be printed in any order, because a `Set` (unlike a `List`) is an unordered collection of values.

```
HashSet set = new HashSet( );
for (int k=1; k<=10; k++) {
    set.add(new Integer(k));
}
Iterator it = set.iterator( );
while (it.hasNext()) {
    Integer tmp = (Integer)it.next( );
    System.out.println(tmp.intValue( ));
}
```

A `for-loop` could also be used instead of the `while-loop` used in the code given above:

```
for (Iterator it = set.iterator(); it.hasNext();) {
    Integer tmp = (Integer)it.next();
    System.out.println(tmp.intValue());
}
```

Note that the *update-expression* part of this `for-loop` is empty. That is because the call to `it.next` inside the loop not only returns the next value in the set but also "advances" the iterator.

Below is some code that illustrates the use of the `remove` method. Assume that variable `s` is a `Set` of `Strings`. The code finds all strings in the set that start with an "x" and removes those strings from the set.

```
for (Iterator it = s.iterator(); it.hasNext();) {
    String tmp = (String)it.next( );
    if (tmp.length() > 0) {
        tmp = tmp.substring(0,1);
        if (tmp.equals("x")) it.remove( );
    }
}
```

The `ListIterator` interface is an extension of the `Iterator` interface. It is used when the collection of objects being iterated over is a `List`.

The AP CS Java subset includes the following additional methods for the `ListIterator` interface:

Method	Explanation
`void add(Object x)`	Inserts x into the list immediately before the element that would be returned by `next` (if there is no such element, inserts x at the end of the list).
`void set(Object x)`	Replaces the last element returned by `next` with x (throws an exception if there is no such element).

Below is some code that illustrates the use of the `set` method. Assume that variable `L` is a list of strings. The code replaces each instance of the string "x" with the string "a".

```
for (ListIterator it = L.listIterator(); it.hasNext();) {
    String tmp = (String)it.next();
    if (tmp.equals("x") {
        it.set("a");
    }
}
```

3.2.2   The *ap.java.util.List* Interface (AB only)

This interface is used for sequences of objects (possibly containing duplicates). For example, the `LinkedList` and `ArrayList` classes both implement the `List` interface.

The AP CS Java subset includes the following `List` methods:

Method	Explanation
`void add(Object x)`	Adds x to the end of this list.
`Object get(int n)`	If index n is out of bounds (n < 0 or n >= size()), throws an `IndexOutOfBoundsException`. Otherwise, returns the element at position n (counting from zero) in this list.
`Iterator iterator())`	Returns an iterator for this list.
`ListIterator listIterator()`	Returns a list iterator for this list.
`Object set(int n, Object x)`	If index n is out of bounds (n < 0 or n >= size()), throws an `IndexOutOfBoundsException`. Otherwise, replaces the element at position n (counting from zero) in this list with x and returns the object that was previously at position n.
`int size()`	Returns the number of elements in this list.

Note that there are three ways to iterate through a `List`, accessing each item in turn: using the `get` method, using the `iterator` method, or using the `listIterator` method. Here are three loops to illustrate each possibility (assume that variable `L` is a `List`); each loop prints the items in the list in the order in which they are stored in the list:

```
for (int k=0; k<L.size(); k++) {
    System.out.println(L.get(k));
}

for (Iterator it = L.iterator(); it.hasNext();) {
    System.out.println(it.next());
}

for (ListIterator it = L.listIterator(); it.hasNext();) {
    System.out.println(it.next());
}
```

3.2.3   The *ap.java.util.Map* Interface (AB only)

This interface is used for sets of objects, each with an associated unique key. For example, the `HashMap` and `TreeMap` classes both implement the `Map` interface.

The AP CS Java subset includes the following `Map` methods:

Method	Explanation
`boolean containsKey(Object key)`	Returns `true` if this map contains `key`; otherwise, returns `false`.
`Object get(Object key)`	Returns the value associated with `key` in this map. Returns `null` if this map does not contain `key`.
`Set keySet()`	Returns a set view of the keys contained in this map.
`Object put(Object key, Object val)`	If this map already contains value `val` associated with `key`, then does nothing and returns `null`. Otherwise, if this map already contains a value v associated with `key`, then replaces it with `val` and returns v. Otherwise, adds `val` to the map associated with `key` and returns `null`.
`Object remove(Object key)`	Removes the mapping for `key` from this map if it is there, and returns the value previously associated with `key` (returns `null` if `key` was not in the map).
`int size()`	Returns the number of key-value mappings in this map.

3.2.4 The *ap.java.util.Set* Interface (AB only)

This interface is used for sets of objects (with no duplicates, and in no particular order). For example, the `HashSet` and `TreeSet` classes both implement the `Set` interface.

The AP CS Java subset includes the following `Set` methods:

Method	Explanation
`boolean add(Object x)`	Adds x to this set if it is not already there. Returns `true` if x was not already in this set; otherwise, returns `false`.
`boolean contains(Object x)`	Returns `true` if this set contains x; otherwise, returns `false`.
`Iterator iterator()`	Returns an iterator for this set.
`boolean remove(Object x)`	Removes x from this set if it is there. Returns `true` if x was in this set; otherwise, returns `false`.
`int size()`	Returns the number of elements in this set.

3.2.5 The *ap.java.util.ArrayList* Class

The `ArrayList` class implements the `ap.java.util.List` interface (described above in Section 3.2.2). An instance of the `ArrayList` class represents a list of Objects (i.e., an ordered sequence). Like an array, elements can be accessed using their position in the list. The AP CS Java subset includes the following `ArrayList` methods (AB students: see Section 3.2.1 for more about iterators):

Method	Explanation
`boolean add(Object x)`	Adds x to the end of this list and returns `true`.
`void add(int n, Object x)`	If index n is out of bounds (`n < 0` or `n > size()`), throws an `IndexOutOfBoundsException`. Otherwise, moves the elements in positions n (counting from zero) to the end of this list over one place to the right to make room for new element x, then inserts x at position n in this list.

Method	Explanation
`Object get(int n)`	If index n is out of bounds (n < 0 or n >= size()), throws an `IndexOutOfBoundsException`. Otherwise, returns the element at position n (counting from zero) in this list.
`Iterator iterator()` (AB only)	Returns an iterator for this list.
`ListIterator listIterator()` (AB only)	Returns a list iterator for this list.
`Object remove(int n)`	If index n is out of bounds (n < 0 or n >= size()), throws an `IndexOutOfBoundsException`. Otherwise, removes the element at position n (counting from zero) in this list, then shifts the remaining elements over one place to the left to fill in the gap. Returns the removed element.
`void set(int n, Object x)`	If index n is out of bounds (n < 0 or n >= size()), throws an `IndexOutOfBoundsException`. Otherwise, replaces the element at position n (counting from zero) in this list with x.
`int size()`	Returns the number of elements in this list.

One advantage of an `ArrayList` compared to a plain array is that whereas the size of an array is fixed when it is created (e.g., `int[] A = new int[10];` creates an array of integers of size 10), the size of an `ArrayList` can change: the size increases by one each time a new item is added (using either version of the `add` method), and the size decreases by one each time an item is removed (using the `remove` method).

One disadvantage of an `ArrayList` compared to a plain array is that whereas a plain array can contain any type of item, an `ArrayList` can only contain `Object`s; in particular, it cannot contain `int`s or `double`s.

3.2.6 The *ap.java.util.HashMap* and *ap.java.util.TreeMap* Classes (AB only)

The HashMap class and the TreeMap class both implement the ap.java.util.Map interface (described above in Section 3.2.3). Instances of these classes represent sets of objects, each with a unique key and some associated information. The AP CS Java subset includes the following methods for the two classes:

Method	Explanation
`boolean containsKey(Object key)`	Returns `true` if this map contains key; otherwise, returns `false`.
`Object get(Object key)`	Returns the value associated with key in this map. Returns `null` if this map does not contain key.
`Set keySet()`	Returns a set view of the keys contained in this map.
`Object put(Object key, Object val)`	If this map already contains value val associated with key, then does nothing and returns `null`. Otherwise, if this map already contains a value v associated with key, then replaces it with val and returns v. Otherwise, adds val to the map associated with key and returns `null`.
`int size()`	Returns the number of key-value mappings in this map.

The AP standard classes provide a number of different ways to store collections of data. The HashMap and TreeMap classes are two examples. It is usually a good idea to use one of these classes when:

- The data to be stored consist of a unique key plus some associated information.
- Accessing one piece of data based on the value of its key is a common operation.

Although other classes (e.g., a List or Set) could be used, the advantage of the Map classes is that they provide efficient methods to add a new piece of data and to look up a piece of data based on its key (the put and get methods).

For example, a teacher might want to design a data structure to keep track of the homework and exam grades for each of the students in her class. A Map would be a good choice for the data structure, because she could use the students' names as the key values and the lists of grades as the associated information. The Map would allow her to find a particular student's list of grades quickly (using the get method), as well as to add information about a new student quickly (using the put method).

3.2.7 The *ap.java.util.HashSet* and *ap.java.util.TreeSet* Classes (AB only)

The HashSet class and the TreeSet class both implement the ap.java.util.Set interface (described above in Section 3.2.4). Instances of these classes represent sets of objects (with no duplicates, and in no particular order). The AP CS Java subset includes the following methods for the two classes.

Method	Explanation
boolean add(Object x)	Adds x to this set if it is not already there. Returns true if x was *not* already in this set; otherwise, returns false.
boolean contains(Object x)	Returns true if this set contains x; otherwise, returns false.
Iterator iterator()	Returns an iterator for this set.
boolean remove(Object x)	Removes x from this set if it is there. Returns true if x was in this set; otherwise, returns false.
int size()	Returns the number of elements in this set.

A Set, like a Map, provides a data structure that can be used to store a collection of items. A Set is a better choice than a Map when the items to be stored consist only of unique values with no associated information. For example, suppose you want a data structure to keep track of the names of all of the movies you've ever seen, and you plan to implement only the following operations:

- Add a new name to the data structure (each time you see a new movie)

- Look up a name in the data structure (each time you want to know whether you've already seen a particular movie)

In this case, a Set would be a good choice for the data structure, since it provides efficient methods for both operations (the add and contains methods).

3.2.8 The *ap.java.util.LinkedList* Class (AB only)

The LinkedList class implements the ap.java.util.List interface (described above in Section 3.2.2). An instance of the LinkedList class represents a list of objects (i.e., an ordered sequence) that is implemented using a linked list (see Chapter 7 for more about linked lists). The AP CS Java subset includes the following LinkedList methods:

Method	Explanation
boolean add(Object x)	Adds x to the end of this list and returns *true*.
void addFirst(Object x)	Adds x at the beginning of this list.
void addLast(Object x)	Adds x to the end of this list.
Object get(int n)	If index n is out of bounds (n < 0 or n >= size()), throws an IndexOutOfBoundsException. Otherwise, returns the element at position n (counting from zero) in this list.
Object getFirst()	If this list is empty, throws a NoSuchElementException. Otherwise, returns the first element in this list.
Object getLast()	If this list is empty, throws a NoSuchElementException. Otherwise, returns the last element in this list.
Iterator iterator()	Returns an iterator for this list.
ListIterator listIterator()	Returns a list iterator for this list.
Object removeFirst()	If this list is empty, throws a NoSuchElementException. Otherwise, removes and returns the first element in this list.

Method	Explanation
`Object removeLast()`	If this list is empty, throws a `NoSuchElementException`. Otherwise, removes and returns the last element in this list.
`Object set(int n, Object x)`	If index n is out of bounds (n < 0 or n >= size()), throws an `IndexOutOfBoundsException`. Otherwise, replaces the element at position n (counting from zero) in this list with x, and returns the object that was previously at position n.
`int size()`	Returns the number of elements in this list.

3.2.9 The *ap.java.util.Random* class

The `Random` class provides methods for generating pseudorandom numbers. The numbers can be integers (covering the full range of possible integer values) or doubles (in the range 0.0 to 1.0). The AP CS Java subset includes the following `Random` methods.

Method	Explanation
`double nextDouble()`	Returns the next pseudorandom double value between 0.0 and 1.0.
`int nextInt(int n)`	Returns the next pseudorandom integer value between 0 (inclusive) and n (exclusive).

PRACTICE MULTIPLE-CHOICE QUESTIONS

1. Consider writing code to simulate flipping a coin ten times. An outline of the code is given below.

```
Random ran = new Random();
for (int k=1; k<=10; k++) {
    if (expression == 0) System.out.println("heads");
    else System.out.println("tails");
}
```

Which of the following is the best replacement for *expression*?

A. `ran.nextInt(0)`

B. `ran.nextInt(1)`

C. `ran.nextInt(2)`

D. `ran.nextInt(10)`

E. `ran.nextInt(k)`

Questions 2 and 3 assume that variable a is an `ArrayList` that has been initialized to contain a list of ten strings.

2. Which of the following statements correctly adds the string `"the end"` to the end of the list?

<u>Statement I</u>	<u>Statement II</u>	<u>Statement III</u>
`a.add("the end");`	`a.add(10, "the end");`	`a.set(10, "the end");`

A. I only

B. II only

C. I and II

D. I and III

E. II and III

3. Which of the following code segments correctly replaces the first string in the list with the string `"start"`?

A. `a.set(0, "start");`

B. `a.get(0, "start");`

C. `a.add("start");`

D. `a.add(0, "start");`

E. `a.remove(0);`
    `a.add("start");`

Questions 4 and 5 (for AB students only) concern the following situation: Consider writing a program to keep track of information about the students enrolled in a class. The information for each student is the student's (unique) ID number, and the student's name. Assume that variable m is a Map that has been initialized to store the information for the class (using a string that represents the ID number as the key, and another string that represents the student's name as the associated object).

4. (AB only) Which of the following code segments prints the names of all of the students in the class?

A. ```
System.out.println(m);
```

B. ```
System.out.println(m.get());
```

C. ```
for (int k=1; k<m.size(); k++) {
        System.out.println(m.get(k));
}
```

D. ```
Set keys = m.keySet();
for (Iterator it = keys.iterator(); it.hasNext(); ) {
        System.out.println(it.next());
}
```

E. ```
Set keys = m.keySet();
        for (Iterator it = keys.iterator();
                it.hasNext();) {
        Object oneKey = it.next();
        System.out.println(m.get(oneKey));
        }
```

5. (AB only) Which of the following expressions evaluates to true if and only if there is a student with ID number 12345 in the class?

A. ```
m.get("12345")
```

B. ```
m.containsKey("12345")
```

C. ```
m.size() > 0
```

D. ```
m.keySet().iterator().hasNext()
```

E. ```
m.keySet().iterator().next()
```

ANSWERS TO MULTIPLE-CHOICE QUESTIONS

1. C
2. C
3. A
4. E
5. B

ANSWERS TO MULTIPLE-CHOICE QUESTIONS

1. C
2. C
3. A
4. E
5. B

3.3 Interfaces and Classes from the *ap* Package

The interfaces and classes from the *ap* package are discussed in Chapter 6, which also provides practice multiple-choice questions. A summary of the methods defined for each interface and class is given here.

3.3.1 The *ap.PriorityQueue* Interface (AB only)

Method	Explanation
`void add(Object x)`	Inserts x into this priority queue.
`boolean isEmpty()`	Returns true if this priority queue is empty; otherwise, returns false.
`Object peekMin()`	If this priority queue is empty, throws an exception. Otherwise, returns the smallest item in this priority queue without removing it.
`Object removeMin()`	If this priority queue is empty, throws an exception. Otherwise, removes and returns the smallest item in this priority queue.

3.3.2 The *ap.Queue* Interface (AB only)

Methods	
`Object dequeue()`	If this queue is empty, throws an exception. Otherwise, removes and returns the first item from this queue.
`void enqueue(Object x)`	Adds x to the end of this queue.
`boolean isEmpty()`	Returns `true` if this queue is empty; otherwise, returns `false`.
`Object peekFront()`	If this queue is empty, throws an exception. Otherwise, returns the first item in this queue without removing it.

3.3.3   The *ap.Stack* Interface (AB only)

Method	Explanation
`boolean isEmpty()`	Returns `true` if this stack is empty; otherwise, returns `false`.
`Object peekTop()`	If this stack is empty, throws an exception. Otherwise, returns the item on the top of this stack without removing it.
`Object pop()`	If this stack is empty, throws an exception. Otherwise, removes and returns the first item from this stack.
`void push(Object x)`	Adds x to the top of this stack.

3.3.4   The *ap.ListNode* Class (AB only)

Method	Explanation
`ListNode getNext()`	Returns the next node in the list.
`Object getValue()`	Returns the value in this node.
`void setNext(ListNode n)`	Sets the pointer to the next node to n.
`void setValue(Object x)`	Sets the value in this node to x.

3.3.5   The *ap.TreeNode* Class (AB only)

Method	Explanation
`Object getValue()`	Returns the value in this tree node.
`TreeNode getLeft()`	Returns a pointer to this node's left child.
`TreeNode getRight()`	Returns a pointer to this node's right child.
`TreeNode setLeft (TreeNode n)`	Sets the pointer to this node's left child to n.
`TreeNode setRight (TreeNode n)`	Sets the pointer to this node's right child to n.
`void setValue(Object x)`	Sets the value in this node to x.

Quick Reference Guide to AP Computer Science Classes and Interfaces

ArrayList (A and AB)

Constructors	
`ArrayList()`	Creates a new, empty `ArrayList`.
Methods	
`boolean add(Object x)`	Adds x to the end of this list and returns `true`.
`void add(int n, Object x)`	If index n is out of bounds (n < 0 or n > size()), throws an `IndexOutOfBoundsException`. Otherwise, moves the elements in positions n (counting from zero) to the end of this list and over one place to the right to make room for new element x, then inserts x at position n in this list.
`Object get(int n)`	If index n is out of bounds (n < 0 or n >= size()), throws an `IndexOutOfBoundsException`. Otherwise, returns the element at position n (counting from zero) in this list.
`Iterator iterator())` (AB only)	Returns an iterator for this list.
`ListIterator listIterator())` (AB only)	Returns a list iterator for this list.
`Object remove(int n)`	If index n is out of bounds (n < 0 or n >= size()), throws an `IndexOutOfBoundsException`. Otherwise, removes the element at position n (counting from zero) in this list then shifts the remaining elements over one place to the left to fill in the gap. Returns the removed element.
`Object set(int n, Object x)`	If index n is out of bounds (n < 0 or n >= size()), throws an `IndexOutOfBoundsException`. Otherwise, replaces the element at position n (counting from zero) in this list with x, and returns the object that was previously at position n.
`int size()`	Returns the number of elements in this list.

Comparable (A and AB)

Methods	
`int compareTo(Object other)`	Returns a negative integer, zero, or a positive integer depending on whether this `Object` is less than, equal to, or greater than `other`.

Double (A and AB)

Constructors	
`Double(double d)`	Creates a new `Double` that represents d.
Methods	
`int compareTo(Object other)`	If `other` is not a `Double`, throws an exception. Otherwise, returns a negative integer, zero, or a positive integer depending on whether this `Double`'s value is less than, equal to, or greater than `other`'s value.
`double doubleValue ()`	Returns the double represented by this `Double`.
`boolean equals(Object other)`	Returns `true` if `other` is a `Double` with the same value as this `Double`; otherwise, returns `false`.
`String toString()`	Returns a string representation of this `Double`.

HashMap (AB only)

Constructors	
`HashMap()`	Creates a new, empty map (implemented using a hashtable).
Methods	
`boolean containsKey(Object key)`	Returns `true` if this map contains `key`; otherwise, returns `false`.
`Object get(Object key)`	Returns the value associated with `key` in this map. Returns `null` if this map does not contain `key`.
`Set keySet()`	Returns a set view of the keys contained in this map.
`Object put(Object key, Object value)`	If this map already contains value `val` associated with `key`, then does nothing and returns `null`. Otherwise, if this map already contains a value `v` associated with `key`, then replaces it with `val` and returns `v`. Otherwise, adds `val` to the map associated with `key`, and returns `null`.
`int size()`	Returns the number of key-value mappings in this map.

HashSet (AB only)

Constructors	
`HashSet()`	Creates a new, empty set (implemented using a hashtable).
Methods	
`boolean add(Object x)`	Adds x to this set if it is not already there. Returns `true` if x was *not* already in this set; otherwise, returns `false`.
`boolean contains(Object x)`	Returns `true` if this set contains x; otherwise, returns `false`.
`Iterator iterator()`	Returns an iterator for this set.
`boolean remove(Object x)`	Removes x from this set if it is there. Returns `true` if x was in this set; otherwise, returns `false`.
`int size()`	Returns the number of elements in this set.

Integer (A and AB)

Constructors	
`Integer(int k)`	Creates a new `Integer` that represents `k`.
Methods	
`int compareTo(Object other)`	Returns a negative integer, zero, or a positive integer depending on whether this `Integer`'s value is less than, equal to, or greater than `other`'s value.
`boolean equals(Object other)`	Returns `true` if `other` is an `Integer` with the same value as this `Integer`; otherwise, returns `false`.
`int intValue()`	Returns the integer represented by this `Integer`.
`String toString()`	Returns a string representation of this `Integer`.

Iterator (AB only)

Methods	
`boolean hasNext()`	Returns `true` if the collection has more elements; otherwise, returns `false`.
`Object next()`	Returns the next element in the collection.
`void remove()`	Removes the last element returned by the iterator from the collection.

LinkedList (AB only)

Constructors	
`LinkedList()`	Creates a new, empty linked list.
Methods	
`boolean add(Object x)`	Adds x to the end of this list and returns *true*.
`void addFirst(Object x)`	Adds x at the beginning of this list.
`void addLast(Object x)`	Adds x to the end of this list.
`Object get(int n)`	If index n is out of bounds (n < 0 or n >= size()), throws an IndexOutOfBoundsException. Otherwise, returns the element at position n (counting from zero) in this list.
`Object getFirst()`	If this list is empty, throws a NoSuchElementException. Otherwise, returns the first element in this list.
`Object getLast()`	If this list is empty, throws a NoSuchElementException. Otherwise, returns the last element in this list.
`Iterator iterator()`	Returns an iterator for this list.
`ListIterator listIterator()`	Returns a list iterator for this list.
`Object removeFirst()`	If this list is empty, throws a NoSuchElementException. Otherwise, removes and returns the first element in this list.
`Object removeLast()`	If this list is empty, throws a NoSuchElementException. Otherwise, removes and returns the last element in this list.
`Object set(int n, Object x)`	If index n is out of bounds (n < 0 or n >= size()), throws an IndexOutOfBoundsException. Otherwise, replaces the element at position n (counting from zero) in this list with x, and returns the object that was previously at position n.
`int size()`	Returns the number of elements in this list.

List (AB only)

Methods	
`boolean add(Object x)`	Adds x to the end of this list and returns `true`.
`Object get(int n)`	If index n is out of bounds (n < 0 or n >= size()), throws an `IndexOutOfBoundsException`. Otherwise, returns the element at position n (counting from zero) in this list.
`Iterator iterator())`	Returns an iterator for this list.
`ListIterator listIterator()`	Returns a list iterator for this list.
`Object set(int n, Object x)`	If index n is out of bounds (n < 0 or n >= size()), throws an `IndexOutOfBoundsException`. Otherwise, replaces the element at position n (counting from zero) in this list with x, and returns the object that was previously at position n.
`int size()`	Returns the number of elements in this list.

ListIterator (AB only)

Methods	
`void add(Object x)`	Inserts x into the list immediately before the element that would be returned by `next` (if there is no such element, inserts x at the end of the list).
`boolean hasNext()`	Returns `true` if the collection has more elements; otherwise, returns `false`.
`Object next()`	Returns the next element in the collection.
`void remove()`	Removes the last element returned by the iterator from the collection.
`void set(Object x)`	Replaces the last element returned by next with x (throws an exception if there was no such element).

ListNode (AB only)

Constructors	
`ListNode(Object initValue, ListNode initNext)`	Creates a new `ListNode` using the given data value and the given pointer to the next node.
Methods	
`ListNode getNext()`	Returns the next node in the list.
`Object getValue()`	Returns the value in this node.
`void setNext(ListNode n)`	Sets the pointer to the next node to n.
`void setValue(Object x)`	Sets the value in this node to x.

Map (AB only)

Methods	
`boolean containsKey(Object key)`	Returns `true` if this map contains `key`; otherwise, returns `false`.
`Object get(Object key)`	Returns the value associated with `key` in this map. Returns `null` if this map does not contain `key`.
`Set keySet()`	Returns a set view of the keys contained in this map.
`Object put(Object key, Object value)`	If this map already contains value `val` associated with `key`, it does nothing and returns `null`. Otherwise, if this map already contains a value `v` associated with `key`, it replaces `v` with `val` and returns `v`. Otherwise, it adds `val` to the map associated with `key`, and returns `null`.
`Object remove(Object key)`	Removes the mapping for `key` from this map if it is there, and returns the value previously associated with `key` (returns `null` if `key` was not in the map).
`int size()`	Returns the number of key-value mappings in this map.

Math (A and AB)

Methods	
`static int abs(int x)`	Returns the absolute value of `int x`.
`static double abs(double x)`	Returns the absolute value of `double x`.
`static double pow(double base, double exponent)`	Returns the value of `base` raised to the power of `exponent`.
`static double sqrt(double x)`	Returns the square root of `x`.

Object (A and AB)

Constructors	
`Object()`	Creates a new object.
Methods	
`boolean equals(Object other)`	Returns `true` if this `Object` is the same as `other`; otherwise, returns `false`. (Note that the default version returns `true` if and only if the `==` operator returns `true`; i.e., if and only if this `Object` points to the same chunk of memory as `other`.)
`int hashCode()` (AB only)	Returns a hashcode value for this `Object`.
`String toString()`	Returns a string representation of this `Object`.

PriorityQueue (AB only)

Methods	
`void add(Object x)`	Inserts x into this priority queue.
`boolean isEmpty()`	Returns true if this priority queue is empty; otherwise, returns false.
`Object peekMin()`	If this priority queue is empty, throws an exception. Otherwise, returns the smallest item in this priority queue without removing it.
`Object removeMin()`	If this priority queue is empty, throws an exception. Otherwise, removes and returns the smallest item in this priority queue.

Queue (AB only)

Methods	
`Object dequeue()`	If this queue is empty, throws an exception. Otherwise, removes and returns the first item from this queue.
`void enqueue(Object x)`	Adds x to the end of this queue.
`boolean isEmpty()`	Returns true if this queue is empty; otherwise, returns false.
`Object peekFront()`	If this queue is empty, throws an exception. Otherwise, returns the first item in this queue without removing it.

Random (A and AB)

Constructors	
`Random()`	Creates a new pseudorandom number generator, using the current time as the seed.
Methods	
`double nextDouble()`	Returns the next pseudorandom double value between 0.0 and 1.0.
`int nextInt(int n)`	Returns the next pseudorandom integer value between 0 (inclusive) and n (exclusive).

Set (AB only)

Methods	
`boolean add(Object x)`	Adds x to this set if it is not already there. Returns `true` if x was *not* already in this set; otherwise, returns `false`.
`boolean contains(Object x)`	Returns `true` if this set contains x; otherwise, returns `false`.
`Iterator iterator()`	Returns an iterator for this set.
`boolean remove(Object x)`	Removes x from this set if it is there. Returns `true` if x was in this set; otherwise, returns `false`.
`int size()`	Returns the number of elements in this set.

Stack (AB only)

Methods	
`boolean isEmpty()`	Returns `true` if this stack is empty; otherwise, returns `false`.
`Object peekTop()`	If this stack is empty, throws an exception. Otherwise, returns the item on the top of this stack without removing it.
`Object pop()`	If this stack is empty, throws an exception. Otherwise, removes and returns the first item from this stack.
`void push(Object x)`	Adds x to the top of this stack.

String (A and AB)

Constructors	
`String()`	Creates a new, empty string (a string with no characters).
`String(String s)`	Creates a new string with the same sequence of characters as `String s`.

Methods	
`int compareTo(Object other)`	If `other` is not a `String`, throws an exception. Otherwise, returns a negative number if this string comes before `other` in lexicographic order; returns a positive number if this string comes after `other` in lexicographic order; returns zero if the two strings are the same.
`boolean equals(Object other)`	Returns `true` if `other` is a string with the same sequence of characters as this one; otherwise, returns `false`.
`int indexOf(String s)`	Returns the position of the first occurrence of `s` in this string, or -1 if `s` does not occur in this string.
`int length()`	Returns the number of characters in this string.
`String substring(int from)`	Returns the substring that starts with the character in position `from` (counting from zero) and ends with the last character in the string.
`String substring(int from, int to)`	Returns the substring that starts with the character in position `from` and ends with the character in position `to`-1 (counting from zero).

TreeMap (AB only)

Constructors	
`TreeMap()`	Creates a new, empty map (implemented using a balanced tree).
Methods	
`boolean containsKey(Object key)`	Returns `true` if this map contains `key`; otherwise, returns `false`.
`Object get(Object key)`	Returns the value associated with `key` in this map. Returns `null` if this map does not contain `key`.
`Set keySet()`	Returns a set view of the keys contained in this map.
`Object put(Object key, Object value)`	If this map already contains value `val` associated with `key`, then does nothing and returns `null`. Otherwise, if this map already contains a value `v` associated with `key`, then replaces it with `val` and returns `v`. Otherwise, adds `val` to the map associated with `key`, and returns `null`.
`int size()`	Returns the number of key-value mappings in this map.

TreeNode (AB only)

Constructors	

`TreeNode(Object initValue,`
`TreeNode initLeft,`
`TreeNode initRight)`
	Creates a new `TreeNode` using the given data value and the given pointers to the node's children.

Methods	
`Object getValue()`	Returns the value in this tree node.
`TreeNode getLeft()`	Returns a pointer to this node's left child.
`TreeNode getRight()`	Returns a pointer to this node's right child.
`TreeNode setLeft(TreeNode n)`	Sets the pointer to this node's left child to n.
`TreeNode setRight(TreeNode n)`	Sets the pointer to this node's right child to n.
`void setValue(Object x)`	Sets the value in this node to x.

TreeSet (AB only)

Constructors	
`TreeSet()`	Creates a new, empty set (implemented using a balanced tree).
Methods	
`boolean add(Object x)`	Adds x to this set if it is not already there. Returns `true` if x was *not* already in this set; otherwise, returns `false`.
`boolean contains(Object x)`	Returns `true` if this set contains x; otherwise, returns `false`.
`Iterator iterator()`	Returns an iterator for this set.
`boolean remove(Object x)`	Removes x from this set if it is there. Returns `true` if x was in this set; otherwise, returns `false`.
`int size()`	Returns the number of elements in this set.

4

Design and Analysis of Data Structures and Algorithms

4.1 Overview

Designing good data structures and algorithms is a very important part of programming. Data structure design includes defining the set of operations that will be available to the users of the data structure (the *interface*), as well as designing the way the data will actually be stored (the *implementation*). A data structure should be designed with the following goals in mind:

- The code that uses the data structure should be easy to understand.
- The data structure should be easy to modify (for example, by adding new operations).
- The code that implements the data structure should be reasonably efficient.

When designing data structures and algorithms, it is important to consider their space and time requirements (how much computer memory will be required to store the data, and how the running time of each operation is related to the amount of data). Computer Science A students should be able to compare the space and time requirements of different designs, and Computer Science AB students should be able to express those requirements using Big-O notation.

4.2 Big-O Notation (AB only)

Big-O notation is used to express how the space or time required by a particular implementation is related to the amount of data being processed. The table below gives some of the most common Big-O expressions, with explanations and examples.

Expression	Explanation	Example
$O(1)$	Constant. The amount of space or time is independent of the amount of data. If the amount of data doubles, the amount of space or time will stay the same.	An item can be added to the beginning of a linked list in constant time (independent of the number of items already in the list).
$O(\log N)$	Logarithmic. If the amount of data doubles, the amount of space or time will increase by one.	The worst-case time for binary search is logarithmic in the size of the array.
$O(N)$	Linear. If the amount of data doubles, the amount of space or time will also double.	The time needed to print all of the values stored in an array is linear in the size of the array.
$O(N^2)$	Quadratic. If the amount of data doubles, the amount of space or time will quadruple.	The amount of space needed to store a two-dimensional, square array is quadratic in the number of rows.
$O(2^N)$	Exponential. If the amount of data increases by one, the amount of space or time will double.	The number of moves required to solve the Towers of Hanoi puzzle is exponential in the number of disks used.

PRACTICE MULTIPLE-CHOICE QUESTIONS

Questions 1 and 2 refer to the following information:

A farmer has N barns. Each barn contains cows, sheep, or pigs. The farmer wants a data structure to record the following information for each barn:

- The day of the year the animals in the barn were purchased (a number in the range 1 to 365)
- The kind of animals in the barn
- The number of animals in the barn

The farmer plans to define a class named `Barn` to hold information about one barn, and to use an array of `Barn`s of length N to store information about each of the N barns.

The farmer is considering two possible ways to define the fields of the `Barn` class:

Definition 1: Use three fields of type `int`, `String`, and `int` to hold the three pieces of information for each barn.
Definition 2: Use one field that is an `int` array of length 3. The three elements of the array will hold the three pieces of information for each barn.

1. Which of the following is the best reason for preferring Definition 1 over Definition 2?

    A. Definition 2 will not work, since the kind of animal in the barn cannot be represented using an integer.

    B. Less space will be used by Definition 1 than by Definition 2.

    C. Less time will be needed to determine the number of animals in a given barn using Definition 1 than using Definition 2.

    D. Using three named fields, rather than a single array, makes it clearer how the data are to be stored in each instance of a `Barn`.

    E. Since the information about all N barns is to be stored in an array, it is better not to use an array in the definition of the `Barn` class.

2. (AB only) Assume that Definition 1 has been chosen. Which of the following best characterizes the time needed to print all of the information about the kth barn?

    A. O(1)

    B. O(k)

    C. O(log N)

    D. O($k * N$)

    E. O(N^2)

Questions 3 and 4 refer to the following information:

A teacher needs a data structure to store information about student absences each day of the 80-day semester. There are N students in the class. Two different designs are being considered.

Design 1: A one-dimensional array with 80 elements. Each element of the array is an array of N strings. Each string is either "absent" or "present."

Design 2: A two-dimensional array with 80 rows and N columns. Each element of the array contains a boolean value (`true` or `false`).

Assume that more space is required to store a string than to store a boolean value.

3. Which of the following statements about the space requirements of the two designs is true?

    A. Design 1 will require more space than Design 2.
    B. Design 2 will require more space than Design 1.
    C. Designs 1 and 2 will require the same amount of space.
    D. Which design will require more space depends on how many students are actually absent during the semester.
    E. Which design will require more space depends on the value of N.

4. Assume that Design 2 is chosen and that the following operation is implemented as efficiently as possible.

    Given a student number j (between 1 and N) and a day number k (between 1 and 80), look in the data structure to see whether student j was absent on day k.

    Which of the following statements is true?

    A. The time required to perform the operation is proportional to the size of the array.
    B. The time required to perform the operation is proportional to the number of students absent on the given day.
    C. The time required to perform the operation is proportional to the total number of students.
    D. The time required to perform the operation is proportional to the number of days in the semester.
    E. The time required to perform the operation is independent of the number of students absent on the given day, the total number of students, and the number of days in the semester.

5. (AB only) Consider the following code segment:

```
int N = some positive integer value;
for (int k=1; k<=N; k++) {
    for (int j=1; j<=k; j++) {
        System.out.print("*");
    }
}
```

Which of the following best characterizes the number of stars printed when this code segment executes?

A. $O(1)$

B. $O(\log N)$

C. $O(N)$

D. $O(N^2)$

E. $O(2^N)$

ANSWERS TO MULTIPLE-CHOICE QUESTIONS

1. D
2. A
3. A
4. E
5. D

5

Sorting and Searching

5.1 Sorting

Both A and AB students should be familiar with a number of sorting algorithms. Students should understand that some algorithms are more efficient than others, and they should be able to reason about the efficiency of an algorithm, given a description of how it works.

This section is divided into two parts. The first part reviews two quadratic sorting algorithms: Selection Sort and Insertion Sort. The second part reviews two more efficient algorithms: Quick Sort and Merge Sort. In all cases, it is assumed that the values to be sorted are in an array.

5.1.1 Quadratic Sorting Algorithms

Selection Sort

Selection Sort works by finding the smallest element in the array and swapping it with the value in the first position, then finding the second smallest element and swapping it with the value in the second position, and so on. If there are N values to be sorted, Selection Sort will make N passes through the array of values. The first time, it will look at all N values; the second time, it will look at $N - 1$ values; the third time, it will look at $N - 2$ values; and so on. So the time required by Selection Sort is proportional to:

$$N + (N - 1) + (N - 2) + \ldots + 3 + 2 + 1$$

This is proportional to N^2. If the values in the array are already in sorted order, Selection Sort will still make the same passes through the array (although it will not do any swaps). Therefore, the time for Selection Sort is proportional to N^2 regardless of how close to sorted the values are initially.

Insertion Sort

Insertion Sort works by making one pass through the array of values; each time it considers an element, it goes *back* through the array to find the appropriate place for that element. In the worst case (when the array of values is initially in *reverse* sorted order), it will have to go all the way back to the beginning of the array every time it considers an element.

In that case, for the first element it will look at 0 previous values; for the second element, it will look at 1 previous value; for the third element, it will look at 2 previous values; and so on. So the time required by Insertion Sort in this case is proportional to:

$$0 + 1 + 2 + \ldots + (N - 2) + (N - 1)$$

Again, this is proportional to N^2.

However, in the best case (when the array of values is already in sorted order), Insertion Sort will only look at one previous value each time it moves on to the next element. In this case, it will only require time proportional to N.

5.1.2 More Efficient Sorting Algorithms

Quick Sort

Quick Sort starts by partitioning the array around a "pivot" value, so that all values that are less than or equal to the pivot come before the values that are greater than the pivot. For example, assume that the array initially contains the following values:

```
4   6   7   0   3   9   3   6
```

If 4 is chosen as the pivot value, then after partitioning, the array might look like this (with the pivot value shown in bold):

```
3   3   0   4   7   9   6   6
```

After partitioning the array, Quick Sort makes two recursive calls: the first call sorts the portion of the array that contains values less than or equal to the pivot, and the second call sorts the rest of the array. The recursion ends when there is just one value to be sorted.

The efficiency of Quick Sort depends on the choice of the pivot value. It is least efficient when the value chosen as the pivot is either the smallest or the largest value in the array. In that case, Quick Sort requires time proportional to N^2 (i.e., it is no more efficient than Selection Sort or Insertion Sort). However, if the number of values that are less than or equal to the pivot is about the same as the number of values greater than the pivot, then Quick Sort is much more efficient. AB students should realize that, in this case, Quick Sort takes $O(N \log N)$ time.

Merge Sort

Merge Sort works by recursively sorting the two halves of the given array into some auxiliary data structures (e.g., two other arrays, each half the size of the original array) and then merging the sorted values back into the original array. (As for Quick Sort, the recursion ends when there is just one value to be sorted.) For example, assume that the array initially contains the following eight values:

```
4   6   7   0   3   9   3   6
```

The first recursive call would sort the left half of the array, producing the following sorted array (of size four):

```
0   4   6   7
```

And the second recursive call would produce the following sorted array:

```
3   3   6   9
```

The two sorted arrays would be merged to produce the following final array:

```
0   3   3   4   6   6   7   9
```

AB students should recognize that Merge Sort requires $O(N \log N)$ time. A students should simply understand that Merge Sort is always more efficient than Selection Sort and usually more efficient than Insertion Sort (except when the array is already sorted or is close to being sorted). However, a disadvantage of Merge Sort is that it requires more space than the other sorting algorithms, because of the auxiliary data structures that it uses.

5.2   Searching

All AP Computer Science students should understand how to search for a given value in an array using sequential or binary search. In addition, AB students should understand searching using a hashtable and using a binary search tree. Sequential search, binary search, and hashing are reviewed below; binary search trees are discussed in Chapter 8.

Sequential Search

A *sequential search* simply involves looking at each item in the array in turn until either the value being searched for is found or it can be determined that the value is not in the array. If the array is unsorted, then it is necessary to keep searching as long as the value is not found. However, if the array is sorted, it may be possible to quit searching without examining all of the elements in the array. If the array is sorted from low to high, the search can stop as soon as the current array value is greater than the value being searched for.

In the worst case, a sequential search will require looking at the whole array, so the time required to search an array of size N is proportional to N.

Binary Search

If the array is sorted, a *binary search* can be performed and is usually more efficient than a sequential search. A binary search first looks at the middle element, m. If m matches the value being searched for, the search is finished. Otherwise, if m is greater than the value being searched for, we know that if the value being searched for is in the array at all, it must be to the left of m in the array. A new binary search is done on the half of the array to the left of m. Similarly, if m is less than the value being searched for, we know that if the value being searched for is in the array at all, it must be to the right of m in the array. A new binary search is done on the half of the array to the right of m. If the value being searched for is not in the array, a new binary search will eventually be done on an array of size zero. At that point, the search will end (knowing that the value being searched for was not in the original array).

Binary search is proportional to the log (base 2) of the size of the array.[1] AB students should recognize that the worst-case time for binary search is $O(\log N)$.

Hashing (AB only)

Hashing is used to provide a data structure (called a *hashtable*) that supports both fast insert and look-up operations. Although we can look up a value in a sorted array of size N in $O(\log N)$ time using binary search, inserting a new value into the array—keeping it sorted— can require $O(N)$ time. In contrast, insertion into a hashtable can be done in constant time, and (with some care) a look-up in a hashtable can also be done in constant time.

In order to store values in a hashtable, a *hash function* that maps values to integers is required (that is, the function takes a value as its parameter and returns the corresponding integer). The hash function tells which element of the hashtable (which is an array) will hold the value, so the integer that it returns must be in the range 0 to $k - 1$, where k is the size of the array. Although the values can be stored directly in the hashtable, a better approach is to make each element of the hashtable a linked list and to store the values as the list elements.

To insert a value v into a hashtable, the hash function is applied to v, returning an integer k, and then v is added to the front of the list that is in the kth element of the hashtable. Since a value can be added to the front of a linked list in constant time, the time for the insert operation is independent of the number of values already in the hashtable. If the hash function is $O(1)$, then the time for the insert operation is also $O(1)$.

To look up value v, the hash function is applied to v, returning integer k, and then the list in the kth element of the hashtable is searched. If the hashtable is sufficiently large and if the hash function distributes the values evenly, then no list will contain more than one value, and the look-up operation will be independent of the number of values in the hashtable. Given these assumptions, if the hash function is $O(1)$, then the time for the look-up operation is also $O(1)$. However, if the hashtable is of a fixed, small size and/or the hash function does not distribute the values evenly, then the time to look up a value in a hashtable that contains N values can be as bad as $O(N)$.

Below is an example that illustrates using a hashtable to store names. In this example, the hashtable is an array of size 5; each element of the hashtable is a linked list of names. The hash function first finds the middle letter of the name (if the name has an even number of letters, the hash function uses the letter to the left of the middle). It then computes the position of that letter in the alphabet (1 for a, 2 for b, and so on), and returns the

---

[1] The log base 2 of N is the number of doublings it takes to get N, starting with 1. For example, the log of 2 is 1, because only one doubling is required: one times two equals two. The log of 8 is 3, because three doublings are required: one times two equals two, two times two equals four, and four times two equals eight.

position mod 5. For example, given the name Ellen, the hash function would return 2, because the middle letter of Ellen is l, which is the twelfth letter in the alphabet, and 12 mod 5 = 2.

The names to be inserted into the hashtable are:

```
Ellen    Ann    George    Fred    Susan
```

The corresponding hash values (the integers returned by the hash function) are:

```
2    4    0    3    4
```

After inserting the first four names, the hashtable looks like this:

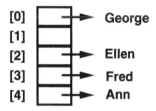

The name Susan hashes to the same place as the name Ann, so after inserting Susan the hashtable looks like this:

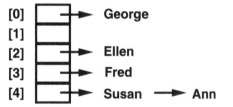

In Java, every Object has a hashCode method, which can be used as that Object's hash function. The hashCode method should guarantee both of the following:

- If an Object's hashCode method is called more than once during the execution of a Java program, the same integer value is returned every time.
- If two Objects are equal according to the equals method, then the same integer value is returned by the hashCode methods of the two Objects.

If you define a class and you want to permit instances of that class to be stored in a hashtable, then you should redefine the hashCode method for the class so that it provides the two guarantees given above.

PRACTICE MULTIPLE-CHOICE QUESTIONS

1. Consider searching for a given value in an array. Which of the following must be true in order to use binary search?

    I.   The values in the array must be integers.
    II. The values in the array must be in sorted order.
    III. The array must not contain any duplicate values.

    A. I only

    B. II only

    C. I and II only

    D. II and III only

    E. I, II, and III

2. Consider searching for a given value in a sorted array. Under which of the following circumstances will sequential search be *faster* than binary search?

    A. The value is not in the array.

    B. The value is in the first element of the array.

    C. The value is in the last element of the array.

    D. The value is in the middle element of the array.

    E. Sequential search will never be faster than binary search.

Questions 3 and 4 refer to the following code segment (line numbers are included for reference). Assume that variable A is an array of `ints` of length N.

```
1. for (int k=0; k<N; k++) {
2.     for (int j=k+1; j<N; j++) {
3.         if (A[j] < A[k]) {
4.             swap(A, j, k);
5.         }
6.         System.out.println(k);
7.     }
8. }
```

3. Assume that `swap` correctly swaps the jth and k^{th} values in array A. Which of the following assertions is true every time line 6 is executed?

    A. The values in array A are sorted from low to high.

    B. The values in A[k] through A[N] are sorted from low to high.

    C. The values in A[k] through A[N] are sorted from high to low.

    D. The values in A[0] through A[k] are sorted from low to high.

    E. The values in A[0] through A[k] are sorted from high to low.

4. (AB only) Assume that `swap` takes constant time. Which of the following best characterizes the runtime of the entire code segment?

   A. O(1)

   B. O(log N)

   C. O(N)

   D. O(N log N)

   E. O(N^2)

5. (AB only) Consider implementing a hash function called `hash` for a hashtable of size N. The values to be stored in the hashtable are strings. Which of the following should be true of the value returned by the call `hash("hello")`?

   A. The value should be in the range 0 to $N - 1$.

   B. The value should be 5, since `"hello"` contains five characters.

   C. The value should be less than the value returned by the call `hash("yellow")`, since `"hello"` comes before `"yellow"` in alphabetical order.

   D. The value should be the same as the value returned by the call `hash("olleh")`, since `"hello"` and `"olleh"` contain the same characters.

   E. The value should be a prime number.

ANSWERS TO MULTIPLE-CHOICE QUESTIONS

1. B
2. B
3. D
4. E
5. A

6

Stacks, Queues, Priority Queues, and Heaps (AB only)

A *stack* is a last-in-first-out collection of objects.

The AP CS exam assumes that students are familiar with the following definition of the Stack interface:

```
public interface Stack {
    boolean isEmpty();
    // postcondition:  Returns true if stack is empty, false
    //                 otherwise.

    void push(Object x);
    // precondition:   stack is [e_1, e_2, ..., e_n] with n >= 0
    // postcondition:  stack is [e_1, e_2, ..., e_n, x]

    Object pop();
    // precondition:   stack is [e_1, e_2, ..., e_n] with n >= 1
    // postcondition:  Throws an unchecked exception if the
    //                 stack was empty.
    //                 Otherwise, stack is [e_1, e_2, ..., e_{n-1}]
    //                 and returns e_n.

    Object peekTop();
    // precondition:   stack is [e_1, e_2, ..., e_n] with n >= 1
    // postcondition:  Throws an unchecked exception if the
    //                 stack was empty.
    //                 Otherwise, returns e_n. (The stack is unchanged.)
}
```

Queues are similar to stacks in that both have operations that add objects to the collection of objects, that remove objects from the collection, that return one object from the collection (without removing it), and that tell how many objects are in the collection; however, a queue is a first-in-first-out collection of objects, whereas while a stack is last-in-first-out.

The AP CS exam assumes that students are familiar with the following definition of the Queue interface:

```
public interface Queue {
    boolean isEmpty();
    // postcondition:  Returns true if queue is empty, false
    //                 otherwise.

    void enqueue(Object x);
    // precondition:   queue is [e₁, e₂, …, eₙ] with n >= 0
    // postcondition:  queue is [e₁, e₂, …, eₙ, x]

    Object dequeue();
    // precondition:   queue is [e₁, e₂, …, eₙ] with n >= 1
    // postcondition:  Throws an unchecked exception if the
    //                 queue was empty.
    //                 Otherwise, queue is [e₂, …, eₙ]
    //                 and returns e₁.

    Object peekFront();
    // precondition:   queue is [e₁, e₂, …, eₙ] with n >= 1
    // postcondition:  Throws an unchecked exception if the
    //                 queue was empty.
    //                 Otherwise, returns e₁. (The queue
    //                 is unchanged.)
}
```

A *priority queue* is a data structure that stores a collection of Comparable objects; that is, objects that implement the Comparable interface, so that they can be compared to determine which is the smallest.

To understand the difference between a priority queue and a "plain" queue, recall that a plain queue is a first-in-first-out collection of objects. This means that if you add N objects to a queue (using the enqueue method) and then you remove N objects from the queue (using the dequeue method), the objects will come out in the same order they went in. By contrast, if you add N objects to a *priority* queue (using the add method) and then you remove N objects from the priority queue (using the removeMin method), the objects will come out in *sorted* order (from low to high).

The AP CS exam assumes that students are familiar with the following definition of the PriorityQueue interface:

```
public interface PriorityQueue {
    boolean isEmpty();
    // postcondition: Returns true if the number of elements in the
    //                priority queue is 0;
    //                otherwise, returns false.

    void add(Object x);
    // postcondition: x has been added to the priority queue;
    //                the number of elements in the priority queue
    //                is increased by 1.

    Object removeMin();
    // postcondition: Throws an unchecked exception if the priority
    //                queue is empty.
    //                Otherwise, the smallest item in the priority
    //                queue is removed and returned, and the number
    //                of elements in the priority queue is decreased
    //                by 1.

    Object peekMin();
    // postcondition: Throws an unchecked exception if the priority
    //                queue is empty.
    //                Otherwise, the smallest item in the priority
    //                queue is returned.  (The priority queue is
    //                unchanged.)
}
```

The AP CS Java subset does not supply implementations of the Stack, Queue, or PriorityQueue interfaces. Questions about these data structures will include code like the following (which defines a class used to represent stacks of Integers):

```
public class IntStack implements Stack {
    implementation omitted
}

Stack s = new IntStack();
```

Students should have experience implementing stacks, queues, and priority queues. For example, an ArrayList or LinkedList can be used to hold the items in the stack, queue, or priority queue.

Students should also be aware that an efficient way to implement priority queues is to use a *heap*(sometimes called a *min-heap*). A heap is a binary tree with two special properties:

1. ***Order Property***: For every node in the tree, the value stored at that node is smaller than all of the values in its subtrees (note that this means that the smallest value is at the root).

2. **Shape Property**: This property has three parts:

  I. Every leaf is either at depth d or $d - 1$ (where the depth of a leaf is the length of the path from the root).
  II. All leaves at depth d are to the left of all leaves at depth $d - 1$.
  III. There is at most one node that has just one child; that child is a *left* child, and it is the *rightmost* leaf at depth d.

Below are some example binary trees; some are heaps and some are not.

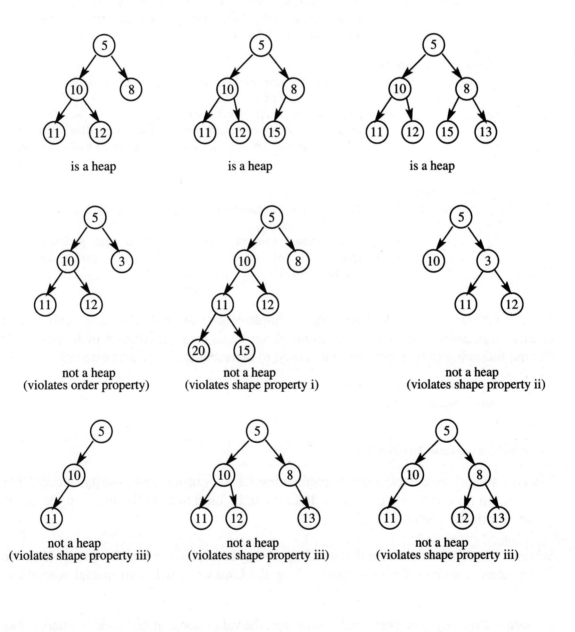

is a heap   is a heap   is a heap

not a heap
(violates order property)

not a heap
(violates shape property i)

not a heap
(violates shape property ii)

not a heap
(violates shape property iii)

not a heap
(violates shape property iii)

not a heap
(violates shape property iii)

A heap is an interesting data structure because two useful operations can be performed in time O(log N), where N is the number of items in the heap:

- Insert a value
- Remove and return the smallest value (so that the binary tree is still a heap)

Clearly, if a heap is used to implement a priority queue, the `add` and `removeMin` operations can be implemented to run in O(N) time (and the other operations can be implemented to run in constant time).

PRACTICE MULTIPLE-CHOICE QUESTIONS

1. Assume that stacks of `Integers` are implemented using the following (incomplete) class definition:

```
public class IntStack implements Stack {
    implementation omitted
}
```

Consider the following code segment:

```
Stack S = new IntStack();
for (int k=1; k<=5; k++) {
    S.push(new Integer(k));
}
while (!S.isEmpty()) {
    System.out.print(S.peekTop() + " ");
    int k = ((Integer)S.pop()).intValue();
    System.out.print(k + " ");
}
System.out.println();
```

What happens when this code segment is executed?

A. A runtime error occurs due to an attempt to pop an empty stack.

B. The while-loop never terminates.

C. The code executes without error; the output is 1 2 3 4 5.

D. The code executes without error; the output is 5 4 3 2 1.

E. The code executes without error; the output is 5 5 4 4 3 3 2 2 1 1.

2. Assume that stacks are implemented by using a linked list to store the items in the stack. How should the push and pop operations be implemented?

	push(Object x)	pop()
A.	add x to the list in sorted order	remove and return the item at the front of the list
B.	add x to the list in sorted order	remove and return the item at the end of the list
C.	add x to the front of the list	remove and return the item at the front of the list
D.	add x to the front of the list	remove and return the item at the end of the list
E.	add x to the end of the list	remove and return the item at the front of the list

3. Consider writing a program to simulate grocery shoppers waiting in check-out lines at a grocery store with ten cash registers. Assume that a Shopper class has been defined (to represent one grocery shopper). Which of the following data structures would be the most appropriate for that program?

A. Ten Shoppers
B. Ten arrays of Shoppers
C. Ten stacks of Shoppers
D. Ten queues of Shoppers
E. Ten linked lists of Shoppers

4. Assume that S is a `String` and that stacks and queues of `Strings` are implemented using the following (incomplete) class definitions:

```
public class StringStack implements Stack {
    implementation omitted
}

public class StringQueue implements Queue {
    implementation omitted
}
```

Consider the following three code segments:

Segment I

```
String newS = "";
for (int k=0; k<S.length(); k++) newS += S.substring(k, k+1);
S = newS;
```

Segment II

```
Stack X = newStringStack();
for (int k=0; k<S.length(); k++) X.push(S.substring(k, k+1));
S = "";
while (!  X.isEmpty()) S += X.pop();
```

Segment III

```
Queue Q = new StringQueue();
for (int k=0; k<S.length(); k++) Q.enqueue(S.substring(k, k+1));
S = "";
while (!  Q.isEmpty()) S += Q.dequeue();
```

Which of these code segments reverses the characters in S?

A. I only

B. II only

C. III only

D. I and II

E. II and III

5. Assume that a priority queue is implemented using a linked list to store the items in the priority queue. The add operation adds the new value at the front of the list, and the peekMin operation looks at all of the values in the list to find (and return) the smallest value.

   Which of the following best characterizes the worst-case running times of the two operations for a priority queue with N items?

	add	peekMin
A.	O(1)	O(1)
B.	O(1)	O(N)
C.	O(log N)	O(log N)
D.	O(log N)	O(N)
E.	O(N)	O(N)

ANSWERS TO MULTIPLE-CHOICE QUESTIONS

1. E
2. C
3. D
4. B
5. B

7

Linked Lists (AB only)

A very useful abstract data type is the *list*: an ordered sequence of values. There are several ways to implement lists; one way is to use a data structure called a *linked list*.

A linked list can be either *singly linked* or *doubly linked*. It addition, the list can be either *circular* or *noncircular*. In all cases, a linked list is a sequence of nodes. Each node contains a value (e.g., in a list of integers, each node would contain an integer) as well as one or more pointers.

In a singly linked, noncircular list, each node contains one pointer, which points to the next node in the list. The last node's pointer is null. In a doubly linked, noncircular list, each node contains two pointers: one pointer points to the next node in the list, and the other pointer points to the previous node in the list. The "next" pointer of the last node in the list and the "previous" pointer of the first node in the list are both null.

In a circular, singly linked list, the "next" field of the last node points to the first node. In a circular, doubly linked list, the "next" field of the last node points to the first node, and the "previous" field of the first node points to the last node.

Below are pictures of four different linked lists that all represent the list of integers: 1, 2, 3, 4, 5.

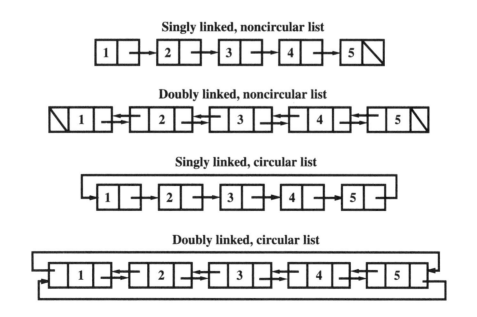

The AP standard classes include a class that implements linked lists: ap.java.util.LinkedList. AB students are expected to be familiar with the following LinkedList operations:

Operation	Description
ListIterator listIterator( )	Returns a ListIterator for the elements in the list.
size()	Returns the number of items in the list.
add(Object x)	Adds Object x to the end of the list.

One way to implement linked lists is to define a ListNode class to be used for each node in the list. The AP CS exam assumes that students are familiar with the following definition of the ListNode class (this definition will be provided in the exam booklet).

```
public class ListNode {
  public ListNode(Object initValue, ListNode initNext) {
      value = initValue;
      next = initNext;
  }
  public Object getValue() { return value; }
  public ListNode getNext() { return next; }
  public void setValue(Object theNewValue) { value = theNewValue; }
  public void setNext(ListNode theNewNext) { next = theNewNext; }

  private Object value;
  private ListNode next;
}
```

Note that the value field of a ListNode has type Object. This allows the ListNode class to be used to implement lists of arbitrary objects; however it means that lists cannot "directly" contain primitive values (e.g., int and double); those values must be "packaged up" using the wrapper classes Integer and Double.

Here is code that creates a singly linked list of ten integers and prints each value in the list in order:

```
ListNode L;          // the first node in the list
ListNode lastNode;   // the last node in the list

// create a list of the integers 1 to 10
L = new ListNode(new Integer(1), null);
lastNode = L;
for (int k=2; k<=10; k++) {
    ListNode newNode = new ListNode(new Integer(k), null);
    lastNode.setNext(newNode);
    lastNode = newNode;
}

// print the values in the list
ListNode tmp = L;
while (tmp != null) {
    System.out.print(tmp.getValue() + " ");
    tmp = tmp.getNext();
}
System.out.println();
```

And here is code that does the same thing, this time using the `LinkedList` class:

```
// create a list of the integers 1 to 10
LinkedList L = new LinkedList();
for (int k=1; k<=10; k++) {
    L.add(new Integer(k));
}

// print the values in the list
ListIterator iter = L.listIterator();
while (iter.hasNext()) {
    System.out.print(iter.next() + " ");
}
System.out.println();
```

Some common operations on linked lists are:

- Add a new node to the front of a list.
- Add a new node to the end of a list.
- Determine whether a list contains a particular value.
- Remove a given node n from a list.
- Given a value v and a node n in a list, add a new node containing v just after node n.
- Given a value v and a node n in a list, add a new node containing v just before node n.

AB students should be able to understand and implement code that performs these and similar operations. This includes understanding the complexity of the operations and understanding which versions of linked lists allow which operations to be implemented more efficiently. For example, given a (pointer to a) node n in a singly linked list that contains N values, removing node n requires $O(N)$ time in the worst case. This is because the list must be traversed, starting with the first node, to find the node that comes immediately before n (because that node's "next" pointer needs to be updated when node n is removed). On the other hand, the same operation can be done in $O(1)$ time in a doubly linked list (because node n includes a pointer to its predecessor).

PRACTICE MULTIPLE-CHOICE QUESTIONS

For questions 1–3, assume that the following method has been added to the standard `ListNode` class (line numbers are included for reference).

```
1. public void printList( ) {
2.     System.out.print(value);
3.     if (next != null) next.printList();
4. }
```

Assume that variable `L` is a `ListNode` and has been initialized as illustrated below:

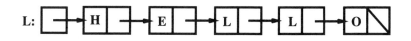

1. What is output as the result of the call `L.printList( )`?

    A. HELLO

    B. OLLEH

    C. HLO

    D. OLH

    E. HHHHH

2. Which of the following best characterizes the running time of method `printList` when it is called for a list containing *N* nodes?

    A. O(1)

    B. O(log *N*)

    C. O(*N*)

    D. O(*N* log *N*)

    E. O(N^2)

3. Assume that lines 2 and 3 of method `printList` are reversed. Now what is output as the result of the call `L.printList( )`?

    A. HELLO

    B. OLLEH

    C. HLO

    D. OLH

    E. HHHHH

4. Assume that a class `MyListNode` has been defined to represent the nodes of some kind of linked list of `Integers`. `MyListNode` has the same methods as the standard `ListNode` class, but you don't know whether it defines nodes for a singly linked or doubly linked list, or whether the list is circular or noncircular.

Assume that the following is a method of the `MyListNode` class:

```
public boolean listMember(Integer K) {
// precondition: this MyListNode is the first node in a
//                linked list
// postcondition: returns true if K is in the list;
//                false otherwise
    if (getValue().equals(K)) return true;
    MyListNode n = getNext();
    while (n != null) {
        if (n.getValue().equals(K)) return true;
        n = n.getNext();
    }
    return false;
}
```

For which of the following kinds of linked lists will method `listMember` work as specified by its pre- and postcondition?

  I.   singly linked, noncircular
  II. doubly linked, noncircular
  III. doubly linked, circular

A. I only

B. II only

C. III only

D. I and II

E. II and III

5. Consider adding the following (incomplete) method to the `ListNode` class:

```
public boolean listEq(ListNode L) {
// precondition:  this node is the first node of a
//                linked list
// precondition:  L is the first node of another linked list
// postcondition:  returns true if the two lists are the same
//                (they contain the same values in the same
//                order); otherwise returns false.
    if ((next == null && L.getNext() != null) ||
        (next != null && L.getNext() == null)) return false;
    if ( condition ) return false;
    if (next == null && L.getNext() == null) return true;
    return expression;
}
```

Which of the following can be used to replace *condition* and *expression* so that method `listEq` works as intended?

	condition	*expression*
A.	`this != L`	`next.listEq(L.getNext())`
B.	`this != L`	`value.listEq(L.getValue())`
C.	`!value.equals(L.getValue())`	`listEq(L)`
D.	`!value.equals(L.getValue())`	`value.listEq(L.getValue())`
E.	`!value.equals(L.getValue())`	`next.listEq(L.getNext())`

ANSWERS TO MULTIPLE-CHOICE QUESTIONS

1. A
2. C
3. B
4. D
5. E

8

Trees (AB only)

Trees are an important abstract data type with many applications in computer science. AB students should be familiar with *binary trees* and with a special kind of binary tree called a *binary search tree*. AB students should also be familiar with *preorder*, *inorder*, and *postorder* traversals of binary trees.

A tree is a collection of nodes and edges. Every nonempty tree includes a special node called the *root*, which has no parent (no incoming edges); every node other than the root has exactly one parent. Every nonempty tree also has one or more *leaves*: nodes with no children (no outgoing edges). A binary tree is a tree in which no node has more than two children. The *height* of an empty tree is 0; the height of a nonempty tree is the number of nodes in the longest path from the root to a leaf. For example:

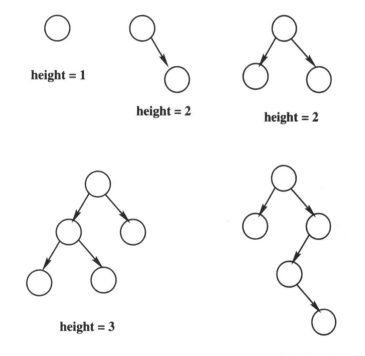

Usually, each node of a tree contains some data (in addition to containing pointers to its children). Binary trees in which the data stored at each node are objects can be implemented as follows (this class definition will be provided in the AP CS exam booklet):

```
public class TreeNode {
    public TreeNode(Object initValue,
                    TreeNode initLeft, TreeNode initRight) {
        value = initValue;
        left = initLeft;
        right = initRight;
    }
    public Object getValue() { return value; }
    public TreeNode getLeft() { return left; }
    public TreeNode getRight() { return right; }
    public void setValue(Object theNewValue) { value = theNewValue; }
    public void setLeft(TreeNode theNewLeft) { left = theNewLeft; }
    public void setRight(TreeNode theNewRight) { right = theNewRight; }

    private Object value;
    private TreeNode left;
    private TreeNode right;
}
```

Preorder, inorder, and postorder traversals of a binary tree all involve visiting all of the nodes of the tree. The difference is the order in which the nodes are visited:

Preorder	Inorder	Postorder
Visit the root;	Visit the left subtree in inorder;	Visit the left subtree in postorder;
visit the left subtree in preorder;	visit the root;	visit the right subtree in postorder;
visit the right subtree in preorder.	visit the right subtree in inorder.	visit the root.

Here is an example of a binary tree of characters and the sequences of characters that would be produced by each of the three traversals:

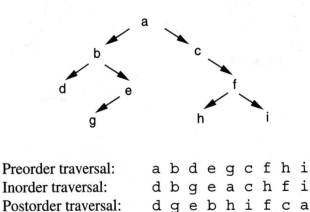

Preorder traversal:	a b d e g c f h i
Inorder traversal:	d b g e a c h f i
Postorder traversal:	d g e b h i f c a

A *binary search tree* is a special kind of binary tree in which, for all nodes n, all data in n's left subtree are less than or equal to the data at node n, and all data in n's right subtree are greater than the data at node n. (It is sometimes useful to consider only binary search trees that contain no duplicate data; in that case, all of the data in n's left subtree are strictly less than the data at node n.)

An advantage of using a binary search tree to store data is that inserting or deleting a value, as well as searching for a value, can be implemented quite efficiently. The average time for each of the operations is O(log N), where N is the number of values in the tree. In the worst case, however, the time for each of the operations is O(N). This happens when the height of the tree is O(N) rather than O(log N); that is, when the tree is tall and skinny instead of short and fat.

Searching for a value v in a binary search tree is similar to performing a binary search in a sorted array. At each step, there is a current subtree to be considered. If the subtree is empty, the search fails. Otherwise, the data d in the root node of the current subtree is examined, and one of three actions is taken:

1. If $d = v$, the search succeeds.

2. If $d > v$, the search continues in the left subtree.

3. If $d < v$, the search continues in the right subtree.

Similarly, in a binary search, at each step there is a current part of the array to be considered. If the current part of the array is empty, the binary search fails. Otherwise, the middle value d in the current part of the array is considered, and one of three actions is taken:

1. If $d = v$, the search succeeds.

2. If $d > v$, the search continues in the left half of the current part of the array.

3. If $d < v$, the search continues in the right half of the current part of the array.

Some common operations on binary trees are:

- Find the largest (or smallest) value in the tree.
- Count the number of nodes, leaves, or nonleaves in the tree.
- Determine the height of the tree.
- Determine whether the tree is a binary *search* tree.
- Compute the sum of the values stored in the tree.

AB students should be able to understand and implement code that performs these and similar operations, and they should understand the complexity of the operations.

PRACTICE MULTIPLE-CHOICE QUESTIONS

1. Assume that the following method has been added to the standard `TreeNode` class.

    ```
    public int treeCount( ) {
        if (left == null && right == null) return 1;
        if (left == null) return right.treeCount();
        if (right == null) return left.treeCount();
        return(left.treeCount( ) + right.treeCount( ));
    }
    ```

    Which of the following best describes what method `treeCount` does?

    A. Always returns 0.
    B. Always returns 1.
    C. Returns the number of nodes in the tree.
    D. Returns the number of leaf nodes in the tree.
    E. Returns the number of nonleaf nodes in the tree.

2. Consider adding a method that returns the smallest value in a binary search tree to the `TreeNode` class. An incomplete version of the method is given below.

    ```
    public Object smallest( ) {
    // precondition:  this node is the root of a binary search tree
        if ( condition ) return(value);
        else return( expression );
    }
    ```

    Which of the following replacements for *condition* and *expression* correctly complete this method?

	condition	*expression*
A.	`left != null`	`0`
B.	`left == null`	`left.smallest()`
C.	`right == null`	`left.smallest()`
D.	`(left == null) && (right == null)`	`left.smallest()`
E.	`(left == null) && (right == null)`	`right.smallest()`

Questions 3 and 4 concern the tree shown below.

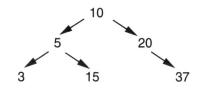

3. Recall that the height of a nonempty tree is the number of nodes in the longest path from the root to a leaf. Which of the following statements about this tree is (are) true?

    I. It is a binary tree.
    II. It is a binary search tree.
    III. Its height is 3.

    A. I only

    B. III only

    C. I and II only

    D. I and III only

    E. I, II, and III

4. Which of the following corresponds to an inorder traversal of this tree?

    A. 3   5 15 10 20 37
    B. 10 5 20 3 15 37
    C. 3   5 10 15 20 37
    D. 10 5 3 15 20 37
    E. 3 15 5 37 20 10

5. Consider the following binary search tree:

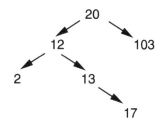

Which of the following could be the order in which the values were inserted into this tree?

    A. −2 12   13 17   20 103
    B. 20 12 103 17   13   −2
    C. 20 12 103 13   −2   17
    D. 103 20   17 13   12   −2
    E. 103 17   −2 13   12   20

ANSWERS TO MULTIPLE-CHOICE QUESTIONS

1. D
2. B
3. D
4. A
5. C

9

Case Studies

Case studies are included in the AP Computer Science curriculum to give students the opportunity to study the development of a nontrivial piece of software; to understand how an expert would go about designing, implementing, and testing such software; and to practice the skills needed to understand and modify code written by someone else.

Each year, the AP Computer Science exams include both multiple-choice and free-response questions about a particular case study. Although a copy of the case study is available to students during the exam, it is absolutely vital that they already be familiar with the case study; there is not enough time during the exam to learn enough about the case study to be able to answer the questions.

If students have not worked with the current year's case study in class, they should obtain a copy from the College Board website or by calling AP Order Fulfillment at: (800) 323-7155.

Because a new case study is released every two or three years, it is not possible to include specific case study material in this review book. We suggest that students use the Addison-Wesley website:

http://www.aw.com/APjava

to access information about the current case study, and to review the following questions about the current case study as part of exam preparation:

- What was the primary goal of the case study?
- What classes were defined, and what are their public methods?
- What constructors were defined for each class, and what do they do?
- What extensions to the code developed in the case study might be useful?
- What aspects of the code might be made more efficient?
- What new methods might be added to the classes defined in the case study?
- What new subclasses might be defined and used in the case study?
- What other applications might use code similar to the code developed for this case study? Which classes and methods could be reused, and what new classes and/or methods would have to be defined?

PRACTICE
EXAMINATIONS

Hints for Students

This section contains a few practical hints that may help you improve your performance on the AP Computer Science exam.

Multiple-Choice Questions

Hint 1

When the multiple-choice questions are graded, one-quarter of a point is subtracted for each wrong answer to compensate for guessing. Therefore, if you have no idea what the answer to a multiple-choice question is, you are probably better off skipping the question than just guessing. However, if you are able to eliminate one or more responses as definitely not the right answer, it is a good idea to make a guess among the remaining responses.

Hint 2

Many multiple-choice questions involve some code. It is usually better to look first at the question itself, rather than studying the code. Knowing what is being addressed by the question (e.g., what does the code do, what value is produced by executing the code on a particular input, or which line of code contains an error) will help you to focus on the important aspects of the code without wasting time trying to understand every detail.

Hint 3

Sometimes multiple-choice questions are grouped: two or three questions are asked about a common "preamble," which might, for example, be a piece of code or an explanation of a choice of data structures. Do not give up on the whole group of questions just because you are not able to answer the first question in the group! The second question may be easier; it may even give you a new insight that will help you answer the first question. (And remember, as suggested in hint 2 above, it is usually best to look at the actual questions before spending a lot of time reading the preamble.)

Free-Response Questions

Hint 1

The criteria for grading the free-response questions are determined by the chief faculty consultant, so some changes may occur from year to year. The current philosophy is that the score for a free-response question depends on whether the code works correctly. Syntactic details, programming style, and efficiency are very minor issues. Leaving out a few semicolons will not affect the score; neither will using one-character variable names. Comments are not necessary; however, including brief comments may help you to organize your thoughts and may make it easier for you to check your work. Unless the question specifically addresses the issue of efficiency, it is better to write simple, clear code than to write complicated, super-efficient code.

Note that code written in a language other than Java will probably receive no credit.

Hint 2

Free-response questions are often divided into several parts, each of which involves writing a method. The instructions for one part of the question may include something like:

> In writing method XXX , you may include calls to method YYY , specified above in Part (a).

It will usually (though not always) be easier for you to write method XXX if you do indeed include calls to method YYY. If it isn't immediately obvious to you how to use method YYY, spend a few minutes thinking about a different approach to writing method XXX that involves calls to YYY. This may save you time in the long run, because the version of XXX that uses YYY may be easier to write than the version you originally thought of.

Hint 3

Free-response questions often start with something like this:

> Write method XXX , as started below.

It is a good idea to look at the method header before you continue to read the question. In particular, look at the names and types of the formal parameters, and the pre- and post-conditions.

Hint 4

If you are asked to write a method with a nonvoid return type, don't forget to return a value of the correct type.

Hint 5 (AB only)

Methods that implement operations on binary trees are almost always easier to write using recursion than using iteration.

A Practice Examination 1

Section I

Time — 1 hour and 15 minutes
Number of questions — 40
Percent of total grade — 50

1. The expression

   ```
   !(a || b)
   ```

   is equivalent to which of the following expressions?

   A. `(a || b)`
   B. `(!a) || (!b)`
   C. `(!a) && (!b)`
   D. `!(a && b)`
   E. `(a || b) && (a && b)`

2. Which of the following statements about Java variables and parameters is true?

   A. A variable must be declared before it is used.
   B. The same variable name cannot be used in two different methods.
   C. Variables used as indexes in `for-loops` must be named `i`, `j`, or `k`.
   D. It is good programming practice to use single letters as the names of all variables.
   E. It is good programming practice to name formal parameters `param1`, `param2`, and so on, so that it is clear where they appear in the method's list of parameters.

Questions 3–5 concern the following (incomplete) definition of the `PosSeq` class, which will be used to represent a sequence of positive integer values. Line numbers for the `search` method are included for reference for question 5.

```
public class PosSeq {
    /*** fields ***/
    private int[] seq;

    /*** methods ***/
    public PosSeq( int seqLength ) { // constructor
        int val;
        seq = new int[seqLength];
        for (int k=0; k<seqLength; k++) {
            System.out.println("Enter a positive number:  ");
            missing code
            seq[k] = val;
        }
    }

    public int getMax() {
    // precondition:  seq.length > 0
        int final = value;
        for (int k=1; k<seq.length; k++) {
            if (seq[k] > final) statement
        }
        return final;
    }

1.    public boolean search(int key) {
2.        int k=0;
3.        while ((k < seq.length) && (seq[k] != key)) k++;
4.        if (seq[k] == key) return true;
5.        return false;
6.    }
}
```

3. The constructor for the `PosSeq` class is supposed to be an *interactive* method that initializes the `seq` field using positive numbers typed in by the person running the program. Assume that the method `readInt` reads and returns one integer value typed in by the user. Which of the following is the best replacement for the placeholder *missing code* in the `PosSeq` constructor?

A. ```
val = readInt();
```

B. ```
val = readInt();
if (val <= 0) val = 1;
```

C. ```
val = readInt();
if (val <= 0) System.out.println("Bad input.");
```

D. ```
val = readInt();
while (val <= 0) {
    val = readInt();
}
```

E. ```
val = readInt();
while (val <= 0) {
    System.out.println("Bad input");
    System.out.print("Enter a positive number: ");
    val = readInt();
}
```

4. Which of the following replacements for *value* and *statement* could be used to complete the `getMax` method so that it returns the largest value in the `seq` array?

| | *value* | *statement* |
|---|---|---|
| A. | 0 | `final = k;` |
| B. | 0 | `final = seq[k];` |
| C. | seq[0] | `final = k;` |
| D. | seq[0] | `final = seq[k];` |
| E. | k | `final = k;` |
```

5. The `search` method was intended to return `true` if and only if the given key value is in the `seq` array. However, the method is not written correctly. Which of the following statements about this method is true?

   A. There will be an error when the method is compiled because the `&&` operator used on line 3 is applied to a nonboolean expression.

   B. The test "`(seq[k] != key)`" on line 3 will cause a runtime error whenever `seq` contains the value `key`.

   C. The test "`(seq[k] != key)`" on line 3 will cause a runtime error whenever `seq` does *not* contain the value `key`.

   D. The test "`seq[k] == key`" on line 4 will cause a runtime error whenever `seq` contains the value `key`.

   E. The test "`seq[k] == key`" on line 4 will cause a runtime error whenever `seq` does *not* contain the value `key`.

6. Consider writing a method whose sole purpose is to write an error message using `System.out.print`. Which of the following best characterizes the choice between making the method's return type `void` and making it `int`?

   A. The return type should be `void` because the method performs an operation and does not compute a value.

   B. The return type should be `int` because that is the default return type for Java methods.

   C. The return type should be `void` because `void` methods are more efficient than `int` methods.

   D. The return type should be `int` because `int` methods are more efficient than `void` methods.

   E. The return type should be `void` because the method does not need to be recursive.

7. Consider the following code segment:

```
int[] A = new int[3];
int[] B;

for (int j=0; j<A.length; j++) A[j] = j;
B = A;
for (int j=0; j<A.length; j++) A[j]++;
for (int j=0; j<A.length; j++) {
    System.out.print(A[j] + " " + B[j] + " ");
}
System.out.println();
}
```

What is printed when this code segment executes?

A. 0 0 1 1 2 2

B. 1 0 2 1 3 2

C. 1 1 2 2 3 3

D. 0 1 1 2 2 3

E. Nothing is printed because the use of B[j] in the print statement causes an `ArrayIndexOutOfBoundsException`.

Questions 8 and 9 refer to the following definition of the `Person` class.

```java
public class Person {
    /*** fields ***/
    private String firstName;
    private String lastName;
    private int age;

    /*** methods ***/
    public Person( String fn, String ln, int a ) { // constructor
        firstName = fn;
        lastName = ln;
        age = a;
    }
    public String getFirstName() { return firstName; }
    public String getLastName() { return lastName; }
    public int getAge() { return age; }
}
```

8. Assume that a variable P has been declared as follows:

    ```java
    Person[] P;
    ```

    and that P has been initialized with data for twenty people. Which of the following correctly tests whether the third person's age is greater than 10?

    A. `P.getAge[2] > 10`

    B. `P.Person[2] > 10`

    C. `P[2].Person.getAge() > 10`

    D. `P[2].getAge() > 10`

    E. `P.Person.getAge[2] > 10`

9. Assume that variables p1 and p2 have been declared as follows:

    ```java
    Person p1, p2;
    ```

    Which of the following is the best way to test whether the people represented by p1 and p2 have the same first name?

    A. `p1 == p2`

    B. `p1.getFirstName().equals(p2.getFirstName())`

    C. `p1.getFirstName() == p2.getFirstName()`

    D. `p1.equals(p2)`

    E. `p2.equals(p1)`

Questions 10 and 11 concern the design of a data structure to store information about which seats on an airplane are reserved. The airplane has N rows (where N is some large number); each row has four seats. Two data structures are being considered:

Data Structure 1:

An array of Rows, where a Row is a class with four boolean fields, one for each seat in the row. The length of the array is N. The fields of the kth element in the array are true if and only if the corresponding seats in row k are reserved.

Data Structure 2:

An array of Reservations, where a Reservation is a class with two integer fields: a row number and a seat number. The length of the array is initially 0. Each time a seat is reserved, a new array is allocated, containing one more element than the previous array; the old array is copied over into the new array, and then the last element of the array is filled in with the newly reserved seat's row and number.

10. Under which of the following conditions does Data Structure 1 require less storage than Data Structure 2?

    A. No seats are reserved.

    B. All seats are reserved.

    C. Only the seats in the first row are reserved.

    D. Only the seats in the last row are reserved.

    E. Data Structure 1 never requires less storage than Data Structure 2.

11. Which of the following operations can be implemented more efficiently using Data Structure 1 than using Data Structure 2?

    Operation I:

    Determine how many seats are reserved.

    Operation II:

    Determine whether all seats in a particular row (given the row number) are reserved.

    Operation III:

    Reserve a seat on a half-full airplane.

    A. I only

    B. II only

    C. III only

    D. I and II

    E. II and III

12. Which of the following statements about a method's preconditions is true?

 A. They must be provided by the writer of the method or the method will not compile.

 B. They are translated by the compiler into runtime checks.

 C. They provide information to users of the method, specifying what is expected to be true whenever the method is called.

 D. They provide information to the writer of the method, specifying how it is to be implemented.

 E. They provide information about the class that contains the method.

13. Assume that variable A is an arrays of ints. Consider the following code segment:

```
boolean flag = false;
for (int k = 0; k < A.length; k++) {
    flag = flag && (A[k] > 0);
}
```

 Which of the following best describes what this code segment does?

 A. Always sets flag to true.

 B. Always sets flag to false.

 C. Sets flag to true if every value in A is positive.

 D. Sets flag to true if any value in A is positive.

 E. Sets flag to true if the last value in A is positive.

14. Consider the following code segment:

```
if (n > 0) n = -n;
if (n < 0) n = 0;
```

This segment is equivalent to which of the following?

A. `n = 0;`

B. `if (n > 0) n = 0;`

C. `if (n < 0) n = 0;`

D. `if (n > 0) n = -n; else n = 0;`

E. `if (n < 0) n = 0; else n = -n;`

15. Consider the following two ways to determine whether the values in array A are in sorted order (from smallest to largest). Assume that A contains N values.

Idea 1:

For each index k between 0 and $N - 1$, check whether all elements with indexes larger than k have values greater than or equal to the value in A[k]; if so, the array is sorted.

Idea 2:

For each index k between 0 and $N - 2$, check whether the value in A[k+1] is greater than or equal to the value in A[k]; if so, the array is sorted.

Which of the following statements about the two ideas is true?

A. Only Idea 1 will work.

B. Only Idea 2 will work.

C. Both ideas will work; the two ideas will be equally efficient.

D. Both ideas will work; Idea 1 will be more efficient than Idea 2.

E. Both ideas will work; Idea 2 will be more efficient than Idea 1.

16. Consider the following recursive method:

```
public static void printStars(int k) {
    if (k>0) {
        printStars(k-1);
        for (int j=1; j<=k; j++) System.out.print("*");
        System.out.println();
    }
}
```

What is output as a result of the call `printStars(4)`?

A. ****
    ***
    **
    *

B. *
    **
    ***
    ****

C. ***
    **
    *

D. *
    **
    ***

E. *
    *
    *
    *

17. A program is being written by a team of programmers. One programmer is implementing a class called `Employee`; another programmer is writing code that will use the `Employee` class. Which of the following aspects of the public methods of the `Employee` class does *not* need to be known by both programmers?

    A. The methods' names
    B. The methods' return types
    C. What the methods do
    D. How the methods are implemented
    E. The numbers and types of the methods' parameters

18. Consider writing a program to be used by a car dealership to keep track of information about the cars they sell. For each car, they would like to keep track of the model number, the price, and the miles per gallon the car gets in the city and on the highway. Which of the following is the best way to represent the information?

    A. Define one class, `Car`, with four fields: `modelNumber`, `price`, `cityMilesPerGallon`, and `highwayMilesPerGallon`.

    B. Define one superclass, `Car`, with four subclasses: `ModelNumber`, `Price`, `CityMilesPerGallon`, and `HighwayMilesPerGallon`.

    C. Define five unrelated classes: `Car`, `ModelNumber`, `Price`, `CityMilesPerGallon`, and `HighwayMilesPerGallon`.

    D. Define five classes: `Car`, `ModelNumber`, `Price`, `CityMilesPerGallon`, and `HighwayMilesPerGallon`. Make `HighwayMilesPerGallon` a subclass of `CityMilesPerGallon`, make `CityMilesPerGallon` a subclass of `Price`, make `Price` a subclass of `ModelNumber`, and make `ModelNumber` a subclass of `Car`.

    E. Define five classes: `Car`, `ModelNumber`, `Price`, `CityMilesPerGallon`, and `HighwayMilesPerGallon`. Make `Car` a subclass of `ModelNumber`, make `ModelNumber` a subclass of `Price`, make `Price` a subclass of `CityMilesPerGallon`, and make `CityMilesPerGallon` a subclass of `HighwayMilesPerGallon`.

19. A programmer wants to include an `if` statement in a program and is trying to choose between the two versions shown below. (Note that the only difference between the two versions is that Version 1 is all on one line, whereas Version 2 is broken up into several lines.)

Version 1

```
if ((x > 0) || (x == y)) { x += y; y *= y; } else { x--; y++; }
```

Version 2

```
if ((x > 0) || (x == y)) {
    x += y;
    y *= y;
}
else {
    x--;
    y++;
}
```

Which of the following best characterizes the choice the programmer should make between the two versions?

A. Version 2 must be chosen; because Version 1 has several statements on one line, it will not compile.

B. Version 1 should be chosen: because the code is all on one line, the compiled code will be more efficient than the compiled code for Version 2.

C. Version 2 should be chosen: because the code is broken up into several lines, the compiled code will be more efficient than the compiled code for Version 1.

D. Version 2 should be chosen: although the compiled code for Version 1 will be more efficient, Version 2 is easier to understand, and that is more important than the efficiency of the compiled code.

E. The compiled code will be equally efficient for both versions; however, Version 2 should be chosen because the code is easier to understand.

20. Consider using binary search to look for a given value in an array of integers. Which of the following must be true in order for the search to work?

    I. The values in the array are stored in sorted order.
    II. The array does not contain any duplicate values.
    III. The array does not contain any negative values.

    A. I only

    B. II only

    C. III only

    D. I and II

    E. II and III

21. Assume that variable A is an array of N integers and that the following assertion is true:

    ```
    A[0] != A[k] for all k such that 1 <= k < N
    ```

    Which of the following is a valid conclusion?

    A. Array A is sorted.

    B. Array A is not sorted.

    C. Array A contains no duplicates.

    D. The value in A[0] is the smallest value in the array.

    E. The value in A[0] does not occur anywhere else in the array.

Questions 22 and 23 refer to the following (incomplete) definition of the Employee class. An Employee object will represent one employee, including the person's name and identification number.

```
public class Employee {
    /*** fields ***/
    private String name;
    private String idNum;

    /*** constructors ***/
    public Employee(String theName, String theIdNum) { ... }
    public Employee(String theName) { ... }
}
```

22. Which of the following is a correct definition of variable emp?

```
I.  Employee emp = "John Smith";
II. Employee emp = new Employee("Ellen Brown");
III.Employee emp = new Employee("John Smith",
                           "023456958991123615211");
```

    A. I only

    B. II only

    C. III only

    D. I and III

    E. II and III

23. Each employee's identification number will be a 20-digit integer. Which of the following correctly explains why the field idNum is a String rather than an int?

    A. Less storage is required for a String than for an int.

    B. An int cannot be used to represent the desired values.

    C. The field name is a String; therefore, idNum must be a String, too.

    D. Although the fields name and idNum can have different types, a constructor that initializes both fields can only be written if they have the same type.

    E. A method to change an employee's identification number can be implemented more efficiently if the field is a String.

24. Consider the following code segment. Assume that method `readInt` reads and returns one integer value.

```
int x, sumNeg=0, sumPos=0;
x = readInt();
while (x != 0) {
    if (x < 0)
        sumNeg += x;
    if (x > 0)
        sumPos += x;
}
if (sumNeg < -8)
    System.out.println("negative sum: " + sumNeg);
if (sumPos > 8)
    System.out.println("positive sum: " + sumPos);
```

Which of the following inputs causes every line of code to be executed at least once?

A. 0

B. 2 4 6 8 0

C. 2 -2 4 -4 0

D. 4 -4 6 -6 0

E. -2 -4 -6 -8 0

25. Assume that a program has been run on an input that caused every line of code to be executed at least once. Also assume that there were no runtime errors and that the program produced the correct output. Which of the following is a valid assumption?

A. If the program is changed only by rearranging lines of code, and then run on the same input, there will be no runtime errors, and the program will produce the correct output.

B. If the program is changed only by removing one line of code, and then run on the same input, there will be no runtime errors, and the program will produce the correct output.

C. If the program is run on a different input, there will be no runtime errors, and the program will produce the correct output.

D. If the program is run on a different input, there will be no runtime errors, but the program might produce incorrect output.

E. None of the above assumptions is valid.

Questions 26 and 27 refer to the following code segment (line numbers are included for reference). Assume that method `readInt` reads and returns one integer value.

```
1.    int x, sum;
2.    x = -1;
3.    sum = 1;
4.    x = readInt();
5.    while (x >= 0) {
6.        if (x > 0) {
7.            sum += x;
8.        }
9.        x = readInt();
10.   }
11.   System.out.println(sum);
```

26. For the purposes of this question, two code segments are considered to be *equivalent* if, when they are run using the same input, they produce the same output. Which line could be removed from the code segment given above so that the resulting code segment is equivalent to the original one?

    A. Line 2

    B. Line 3

    C. Line 4

    D. Line 7

    E. Line 9

27. The code segment given above was intended to read values until a negative value was read and then to print the sum of the positive values read. However, the code does not work as intended. Which of the following best describes the error?

    A. Variable x is not initialized correctly.

    B. Variable sum is not initialized correctly.

    C. Variable x is used before being initialized.

    D. Variable sum is used before being initialized.

    E. The negative value intended to signal end of input is included in the sum.

28. Consider the following code segment:

```
ArrayList L = new ArrayList();
for (int k=1; k<6; k++) {
    if (k%2 == 0) L.add("?");
    else L.add("!");
}
```

Which of the following correctly illustrates the values represented by `ArrayList L` after this code segment executes?

A. ?   ?   ?   ?   ?

B. !   !   !   !   !

C. !   ?   !   ?   !

D. ?   !   ?   !   ?

E. ?   ?   !   ?   ?

29. Consider searching for a given value in a large, sorted array. Under which of the following conditions is sequential search slower than binary search?

A. Always

B. Never

C. When the value being searched for is the first element in the array

D. When the value being searched for is the second element in the array

E. When the value being searched for is the last element in the array

30. Consider the following recursive method:

```
public static void printArray(String[] A, int k) {
    if (k < A.length) {
        printArray(A, k+1);
        System.out.print(A[k]);
    }
}
```

Assume that array A has been initialized to be of length 4 and to contain the values "a", "b", "c", and "d" (with "a" in A[0], "b" in A[1], and so on). What is output as a result of the call `printArray(A,0)`?

A. bcd

B. dcb

C. abcd

D. dcba

E. dddd

31. Assume that a class includes the following three methods:

```
public static int min(int x, int y) {
    if (x < y) return x;
    else return y;
}

public static int min(String s, String t) {
    if (s.length() < t.length()) return s.length();
    else return t.length();
}

public static void testMin() {
    System.out.println(min(3, "hello"));
}
```

Which of the following best describes what happens when this code is compiled and executed?

A. The code will not compile because the types of the arguments used in the call to min do not match the types of the parameters in either version of min.

B. The code will not compile because it includes two methods with the same name and the same return type.

C. The code will not compile because it includes two methods with the same name and the same number of parameters.

D. The code will compile and execute without error; the output will be 3.

E. The code will compile and execute without error; the output will be 5.

32. Which of the following is *not* an example of a good use of comments?

    A. Comments included at the beginning of a method to specify the method's pre- and postconditions

    B. Comments included at the end of every line of a method to explain what that line of code does

    C. Comments included at the beginning of a method to say which of the class's fields are modified by that method

    D. Comments included in a class's constructor to explain how the class object is initialized

    E. Comments included before a loop to say what is true each time the loop is executed

33. Which of the following code segments sets variable sum to be the sum of the even numbers between 1 and 99?

    A.
    ```
    int k, sum = 0;
    for (k=1; k<=99; k++) {
        if (k%2 == 0) sum++;
    }
    ```

    B.
    ```
    int k, sum = 0;
    for (k=1; k<=99; k++) {
        if (k%2 == 0) sum += k;
    }
    ```

    C.
    ```
    int k = 1, sum = 0;
    while (k <= 99) {
        sum += k;
        k += 2;
    }
    ```

    D.
    ```
    int k = 2, sum = 0;
    while (k <= 99) {
        sum++;
        k += 2;
    }
    ```

    E.
    ```
    int k = 2, sum = 0;
    while (k <= 99) {
        k += 2;
        sum += k;
    }
    ```

34. Assume that variable `A` is a *sorted* array of `ints`. Consider the following code segment:

```
boolean flag = false;
for (int k=1; k<A.length; k++) {
    if (A[k-1] == A[k]) flag = true;
}
```

Which of the following best describes when variable `flag` is `true` after this code segment executes?

A. Always

B. Never

C. If and only if array `A` really is sorted

D. If and only if array `A` contains duplicate values

E. If and only if all values in array `A` are the same

35. Assume that variable `A` is an array of `Objects`. Consider the following incomplete code segment:

```
int N = A.length;
for (int k=0; k<N/2; k++) {
    loop body
}
```

Which of the following can be used to replace the placeholder *loop body* so that the code segment reverses the values in array `A`?

A. `A[k]     = A[N-k-1];`
   `A[N-k-1] = A[k];`

B. `A[k]   = A[N-1];`
   `A[N-1] = A[k];`

C. `A[k]   = A[N-k];`
   `A[N-k] = A[k];`

D. `Object tmp = A[k];`
   `A[k]   = A[N-1];`
   `A[N-1] = tmp;`

E. `Object tmp = A[k];`
   `A[k]     = A[N-k-1];`
   `A[N-k-1] = tmp;`

36. Consider the following (incomplete) method:

```
public void changeOb( Object value ) {
    . . .
}
```

Assume that variable k is an int, that variable s is a String, and that variable ob is an Object. Which of the following calls to method changeOb will compile without error?

Call I	Call II	Call III
changeOb(k);	changeOb(s);	changeOb(ob);

   A. I only

   B. II only

   C. III only

   D. I and II only

   E. II and III only

Questions 37 and 38 concern the following recursive method:

```
public int mystery(int k) {
    if (k == 1) return 0;
    else return(1 + mystery(k/2));
}
```

37. What value is returned by the call mystery(16)?

   A. 0

   B. 2

   C. 4

   D. 5

   E. 16

38. Which of the following best characterizes the values of k for which the call mystery(k) leads to an infinite recursion?

   A. No values

   B. All positive values

   C. All nonpositive values

   D. All odd values

   E. All even values

39. Consider the following interface definition:

```
public interface Employee {
    public double getSalary();
    public void setSalary( double newSalary );
}
```

Which of the following is a correct implementation of the Employee interface?

A. ```
public class Person implements Employee {
    public double getSalary;
    public void setSalary;
}
```

B. ```
public class Person implements Employee {
    public double getSalary() { return salary; }
    public void setSalary( double newSalary ) {
        salary = newSalary;
    }
}
```

C. ```
public class Person implements Employee {
    private double salary;

    public double getSalary() { return salary; }
}
```

D. ```
public class Person implements Employee {
    private double salary;

    public double getSalary() { return salary; }
    public void setSalary( double newSalary ) {
        salary = newSalary;
    }
}
```

E. ```
public class Person implements Employee {
    private double salary;

    private double getSalary() { return salary; }
    private void setSalary(double newSalary) {
        salary = newSalary;
    }
}
```
```

40. Which of the following best explains what is meant by `overloading` a method?

    A. Defining another method that does the same thing
    B. Defining another method with the same number of parameters
    C. Defining another method with the same parameter names
    D. Defining another method with the same precondition
    E. Defining another method with the same name but different numbers or types of parameters

A Practice Examination 1

Section II

Time — 1 hour and 45 minutes
Number of questions — 4
Percent of total grade — 50

Question 1

Part (a)

Write method `findZero`, as started below. Method `findZero` should return the index of the first element of array `A` that contains the value zero, starting from position `pos`. If no element of `A` from position `pos` to the end of the array contains the value zero, then `findZero` should return -1.

For example:

Array A					Position pos	Value returned by `findZero(A, pos)`
1	0	2	5	6	0	1
1	0	2	5	6	1	1
1	0	2	5	6	2	-1
1	0	2	0	6	0	1
1	0	2	0	6	1	1
1	0	2	0	6	2	3
1	2	3	4	5	0	-1

Complete method f indZero below.

```
public static int findZero(int[] A, int pos) {
// precondition: 0 <= pos < A.length
// postcondition: returns the smallest index k such that
//                (pos <= k < A.length) and (A[k] == 0),
//                or -1 if there is no such index
```

Part (b)

Write method setZeros, as started below. Method setZeros should find the positions of the first two zeros in its array parameter A, and it should set all of the intervening values (if any) to zero. If A only contains one zero, if it contains no zeros, or if the first two zeros are right next to each other, setZeros should not modify A.

For example:

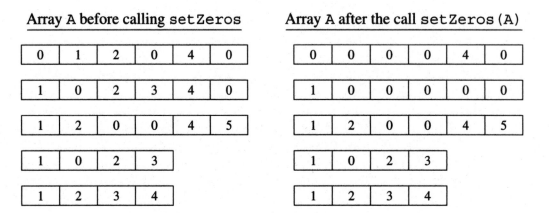

Array A before calling setZeros	Array A after the call setZeros(A)

In writing method setZeros, you may include calls to method findZero specified above in Part (a). Assume that method findZero works as specified, regardless of what you wrote for Part (a).

Complete method setZeros below.

```
public static void setZeros( int[] A ) {
```

Question 2

Consider the following (incomplete) definition of the Time class, used to represent a time of day:

```
public class Time {
    /*** fields ***/
    private int hour;   // a value from 0 to 23
    private int minutes; // a value from 0 to 59

    /*** methods ***/
    public void printTime( ) {
        ...
    }
}
```

The printTime method of the Time class should print the time (using System.out.print) in a 12-hour format, including am or pm as appropriate. Midnight (when both the hour and minutes fields are zero) and noon (when the hour field is 12 and the minutes field is zero) should be treated as special cases; instead of writing the time using numbers, the words midnight or noon should be printed.

For example:

Values of the hour and minutes fields		Output of printTime
hour	minutes	
6	45	6:45am
16	32	4:32pm
0	0	midnight
0	15	12:15am
12	0	noon
12	15	12:15pm
3	0	3:00am
15	5	3:05pm

Note that when the minutes field is less than 10 and it is neither midnight nor noon, *two* digits should be printed after the colon (like "3:00am" and "3:05pm," the last two examples given above).

Complete `printTime` below.

```
public void printTime( ) {
// precondition: 0 <= hour <= 23
//                0 <= minutes <= 59
```

Question 3

Consider the following (incomplete) definition of the `LetterSeq` class, used to represent a sequence of letters:

```
import ap.java.util.ArrayList;

public class LetterSeq {
    /*** fields ***/
        private ArrayList A;     // a list of letters

    /*** methods ***/
        public String listToString( int start, int end ) {
        // precondition: 0 <= start <= end < A.size()
        //               A is a list of Strings, each a single
        //               letter
            ...
        }

        public void printAllWords( ) {
        // precondition:  A is a list of Strings, each a single
        //                letter
        // postcondition: prints all of the English words in A,
        //                each word followed by a space, and
        //                with a newline after all the words

        private static boolean isWord( String S ) {
        // postcondition: returns true if S is an English word,
        //                false otherwise
            ...
        }
    }
```

Part (a)

You will write the `listToString` method of the `LetterSeq` class. Method `listToString` has two integer parameters: `start` and `end`. Method `listToString` should create and return a string containing the letters in A in positions `start` to `end`. (Assume that `start` and `end` have valid values, as specified in `listToString`'s precondition.)

For example, assume that A is as shown below.

Position:	0	1	2	3	4	5	6	7	8	9	10
Letter:	"p"	"r"	"o"	"g"	"r"	"a"	"m"	"m"	"i"	"n"	"g"

Here are some examples of calls to method `listToString`:

Method call	Returned value
listToString(0, 0)	"p"
listToString(0, 2)	"pro"
listToString(6, 7)	"mm"

Complete method `listToString` below.

```
public String listToString( int start, int end ) {
// precondition: 0 <= start <= end < A.size()
//                A is a list of Strings, each a single letter
```

Part (b)

Assume that the `isWord` method of the `LetterSeq` class has been implemented correctly. Write the `printAllWords` method of the `LetterSeq` class. Method `printAllWords` should find all of the English words in A, and it should print them (using `System.out.print` and `System.out.println`) with each word followed by a space and with a newline after all of the words.

For example, assume that A is as shown below.

```
Position:   0    1    2    3    4    5    6    7    8    9
Letter:    "i"  "n"  "o"  "t"  "e"  "b"  "i"  "n"  "d"  "o"
```

A call to `printAllWords` should cause the following to be printed (though not necessarily in this order):

```
i in no not note bin bind i in do
```

In writing method `printAllWords`, you may include calls to method `isWord` (you do not need to write the body of `isWord`). You may also include calls to method `listToString`, specified above in Part (a). Assume that `listToString` works as specified, regardless of what you wrote in Part (a).

Complete method `printAllWords` below.

```
public void printAllWords( ) {
// precondition:  A is a list of Strings, each a single letter
// postcondition: prints all of the English words in A,
//                each word followed by a space, and with a new line
//                after all the words
```

Question 4

This question concerns the two classes, `GroceryStore` and `Product`, partially defined below:

```
import ap.java.util.ArrayList;

public class GroceryStore {
    /*** fields ***/
    private Product[] stock;

    /*** public methods ***/
    public boolean oneSale(String name) {
    // precondition: no two Products in the stock array have the
    //                  same name
    // postcondition: carries out the sale of the named product if
    //                  possible and returns true or false depending
    //                  on whether the sale is successful
        ...
    }

    public ArrayList allSales(String[] orders) {
    // precondition: no two Products in the stock array have the
    //                  same name
    // postcondition: attempts to carry out a sale for each name
    //                  in the orders array, creating and returning
    //                  an ArrayList containing the names of all
    //                  products for which a sale is not successful
        ...
    }

    /*** private methods ***/
    private int findItem(String name) {
    // precondition: no two Products in the stock array have the
    //                  same name
    // postcondition: returns the index of the Product in the stock
    //                  array with the given name, or -1 if there is
    //                  no such Product in the array
        ...
    }
}

public class Product {
    /*** fields ***/
    private String name;
    private int numInStock;

    /*** methods ***/
    public String getName() { return name; }
    public int getNumInStock() { return numInStock; }
    public void sellOne() { numInStock--; }
}
```

Part (a)

Write the `findItem` method of the `GroceryStore` class. As specified by its post-condition, `findItem` should return the index of the `Product` in the `stock` array with the given name, or it should return −1 if there is no such `Product` in the array.

Complete method `findItem` below.

```
private int findItem(String name)
// precondition: no two Products in the stock array have the
//               same name
// postcondtion: returns the index of the Product in the stock array
//               with the given name, or returns -1 if there is no
//               such Product in the array
```

Part (b)

Write the `oneSale` method of the `GroceryStore` class. Method `oneSale` has one parameter: the name of one product (that a customer would like to buy). Method `oneSale` should attempt to carry out the sale of the named product, and it should return `true` or `false` depending on whether the sale is successful. The sale is successful if there is a product in the `stock` array with the given name and if the number of items in stock of that product is greater than zero. In that case, `oneSale` should subtract one from the number of items in stock and return `true`. If there is no product in the `stock` array with the given name or if the number of items in stock for that product is less than or equal to zero, `oneSale` should return `false`.

For example, assume that `stock.length` is 4 and that the elements in the array are as shown below.

	[0]	[1]	[2]	[3]
name:	"milk"	"eggs"	"butter"	"coffee"
numInStock:	20	3	0	1

If `oneSale` is called with the name `"eggs"`, it should subtract one from the number of eggs in stock and return `true`. If `oneSale` is called with the name `"juice"`, it should return `false` (because there is no juice in the `stock` array). If `oneSale` is called with the name `"butter"`, it should return `false` (because there are no butter items currently in stock).

In writing method `oneSale`, you may include calls to method `findItem`, specified above in Part (a). Assume that `findItem` works correctly, regardless of what you wrote for Part (a).

Complete method `oneSale` below.

```
public boolean oneSale(String name) {
// precondition: no two Products in the stock array have the
//               same name
// postcondition: carries out the sale of the named product if
                  possible and returns true or false depending
                  on whether the sale is successful
```

Part (c)

Write the `allSales` method of the `GroceryStore` class. Method `allSales` has one parameter: an array of product names called `orders`. For each name in the `orders` array, `allSales` should attempt to carry out the sale of the named product. It should create a new `ArrayList` containing the names of all products for which a sale is not successful (a product name should appear more than once in the new `ArrayList` if there is more than one failing sale of that product). Finally, it should return the new `ArrayList`.

For example, assume that the `stock` array is initially as shown above in Part (b). Also assume that `allSales` is called with the array of names:

```
  [0]     [1]     [2]     [3]      [4]     [5]    [6]      [7]      [8]
"eggs"  "milk"  "milk"  "butter" "coffee" "tea" "coffee" "milk"  "coffee"
```

Method `allSales` should carry out five successful sales (eggs, milk, milk, coffee, milk), changing the appropriate `Products` in the `stock` array. It should create and return a new `ArrayList` containing the strings

```
"butter" "tea" "coffee" "coffee"
```

because the number of butter items is initially zero, there is no tea product, and the number of coffee items is zero when the second and third attempts to sell one coffee item are made.

In writing method `allSales`, you may include calls to method `oneSale`, specified above in Part (b). Assume that `oneSale` works correctly, regardless of what you wrote for Part (b).

Complete method `allSales` below.

```
public ArrayList allSales(String[] orders) {
// precondition: no two Products in the stock array have the
//               same name
// postcondition: attempts to carry out a sale for each name in the
//                orders array, creating and returning an ArrayList
//                containing the names of all products for which a
//                sale is not successful
```

Answers to A Practice Examination 1

Section I

1.	C	21.	E
2.	A	22.	E
3.	E	23.	B
4.	D	24.	D
5.	E	25.	E
6.	A	26.	A
7.	C	27.	B
8.	D	28.	C
9.	B	29.	E
10.	B	30.	D
11.	E	31.	A
12.	C	32.	B
13.	B	33.	B
14.	A	34.	D
15.	E	35.	E
16.	B	36.	E
17.	D	37.	C
18.	A	38.	C
19.	E	39.	D
20.	A	40.	E

Answers to A Practice Examination 1

Section II

Question 1

Part (a)

Version 1

Use a `for-loop`, exiting the loop using a `return` statement as soon as possible.

```
public static int findZero(int[] A, int pos) {
// precondition: 0 <= pos < A.length
// postcondition: returns the smallest index k such that
//                (pos <= k < A.length) and (A[k] == 0),
//                or -1 if there is no such index
    for (int k=pos; k<A.length; k++) {
        if (A[k] == 0) return k;
    }
    return -1;
}
```

Version 2

Use a `while-loop` whose condition checks both for having reached the end of the array and having found a zero. Note that the order of the expressions in the `while-loop` condition is very important; if it were written like this:

```
(A[k]!=0 && k<A.length)
```

there would be an out-of-bounds array access whenever there was no zero to be found in array A.

```
public static int findZero(int[] A, int pos) {
// precondition: 0 <= pos < A.length
// postcondition: returns the smallest index k such that
//                (pos <= k < A.length) and (A[k] == 0),
//                or -1 if there is no such index
    int k=pos;
    while (k<A.length && A[k]!=0) k++;
    if (k < A.length) return k;
    else return -1;
}
```

Part (b)

```
public static void setZeros(int[] A) {
    int first, second;

    // find the first zero in A
    first = findZero(A, 0);

    // if no zeros or only one zero, quit; otherwise find next zero
    if (first == -1 || first == A.length) return;
    second = findZero(A, first+1);

    // set all elements in the range first+1 - second-1 to zero
    for (int k=first+1; k<second; k++) {
        A[k] = 0;
    }
}
```

Common errors:

- Forgetting to check whether first is −1
- Forgetting to check whether first is the index of the last element of A (omitting this check leads to a call to FindZero that violates its precondition, k < A.length)
- Off-by-one errors (e.g., having the final for-loop index go from first+1 to second)

Note:

It is not necessary to check whether second is −1, because in that case the for-loop executes zero times.

Question 2

Part (a)

Version 1

No auxiliary methods.

```java
public void printTime() {
    if (hour == 0 && minutes == 0) {
        System.out.print("midnight");
    }
    else if (hour == 12 && minutes == 0) {
        System.out.print("noon");
    }
    else if (hour < 12) {
        // am

        // print hour and ":"
        if (hour == 0) System.out.print("12:");
        else System.out.print(hour + ":");
        // print minutes and "am"
        if (minutes < 10) System.out.print("0");
        System.out.print(minutes + "am");
    }
    else {
        // pm

        // print hour and ":"
        if (hour == 12) System.out.print(hour + ":");
        else System.out.print(hour-12 + ":");
        // print minutes and "pm"
        if (minutes < 10) System.out.print("0");
        System.out.print(minutes + "pm");
    }
}
```

Version 2

Use auxiliary methods to convert `hour` and `minutes` to the corresponding strings and to return `"am"` or `"pm"` as appropriate.

```
private String convertHour() {
    Integer h;

    if (hour == 0 || hour == 12) return "12";
    if (hour < 12) h = new Integer(hour);
    else h = new Integer(hour - 12);
    return h.toString();
}

private String convertMinutes() {
    Integer m = new Integer(minutes);
    String s = m.toString();
    if (minutes < 10) s = "0" + s;
    return s;
}

private String amOrpm() {
    if (hour < 12) return "am";
    else return "pm";
}

public void printTime( ) {
    if (hour == 0 && minutes == 0) {
        System.out.print("midnight");
    }
    else if (hour == 12 && minutes == 0) {
        System.out.print("noon");
    }
    else {
        System.out.print(convertHour() + ":" + convertMinutes() +
                            amOrpm());
    }
}
```

Common errors:

- Incorrect handling of times between midnight and 1 A.M. and/or times between noon and 1 P.M. (printing "0" instead of "12")

- Incorrect handling of minutes less than 10 (forgetting to print the necessary extra "0")

- Trying to use auxiliary methods to convert the `hours` and `minutes` fields and making mistakes in converting from an `int` to a `String`

Question 3

Part (a)

```
public String listToString(int start, int end) {
// precondition: 0 <= start <= end < A.size()
//               A is a list of strings, each a single letter
    String S = (String)A.get(start);
    for (int k=start+1; k<=end; k++) {
        S += (String)A.get(k);
    }
    return S;
}
```

Common errors:

- Trying to add characters to the string using indexing instead of string concatenation
- Off-by-one errors on the array index (e.g., using k < end instead of k <= end)
- Forgetting to cast the value returned by A.get to String
- Forgetting to return the string

Part (b)

```
public void printAllWords( ) {
// precondition:  A is a list of strings, each a single letter
// postcondition: prints all of the English words in array A,
//                each word followed by a space, and with a newline
//                after all the words
    String S;
    for (int j=0; j<A.size(); j++) {
        for (int k=j; k<A.size(); k++) {
            S = listToString(j, k);
            if (isWord(S)) {
                System.out.print(S+" ");
            }
        }
    }
    System.out.println();
}
```

Common errors:

- Trying to use a single `for-loop` and calling `listToString` with only one argument
- Using two loops but getting the bounds wrong (e.g., making k start at `j+1` instead of at `j`)
- Forgetting to call `isWord`
- Forgetting to write the final newline
- Writing a newline after every word (instead of only after the last word)

Question 4

Part (a)

```
private int findItem(String name) {
// precondition: no two Products in the stock array have the
//                same name
// postcondition: returns the index of the Product in the stock
//                array with the given name, or -1 if there is
//                no such Product in the array
    for (int k=0; k<stock.length; k++) {
        if (stock[k].getName().equals(name)) return k;
    }
    return -1;
}
```

Common errors:

- Trying to use the private data members of the Product class (e.g., using name directly instead of using the public method getName)
- Using the == operator instead of the equals method
- Forgetting to return −1 for an unsuccessful search

Part (b)

```
public boolean oneSale(String name) {
// precondition: no two Products in the stock array have the
//                same name
// postcondition: carries out the sale of the named product
//                if possible and returns true or false
//                depending on whether the sale is successful
    int k = findItem(name);
    if (k == -1) return false;
    if (stock[k].getNumInStock() <= 0) return false;
    stock[k].sellOne();
    return true;
}
```

Common errors:

- Forgetting to check whether findItem returned −1
- Forgetting to check whether the number of items in stock is greater than zero

Part (c)

```
public ArrayList allSales(String[] orders) {
// precondition: no two Products in the stock array have the
//                same name
// postcondition: attempts to carry out a sale for each name in the
//                orders array, creating and returning an ArrayList
//                containing the names of all products for which a
//                sale is not successful
    ArrayList L = new ArrayList();
    for (int k=0; k<orders.length; k++) {
        if (!oneSale(orders[k])) {
            L.add(orders[k]);
        }
    }
    return L;
}
```

A Practice Examination 2

Section I

Time — 1 hour and 15 minutes
Number of questions — 40
Percent of total grade — 50

1. If addition had higher precedence than multiplication, then the value of the expression

   ```
   2 * 3 + 4 * 5
   ```

   would be which of the following?

   A. 14
   B. 26
   C. 50
   D. 70
   E. 120

2. Assume that x, y, and z are all `int` variables. Consider the following code segment:

   ```
   if (x == 0) {
       if (y == 1) z += 2;
   }
   else {
       z += 4;
   }
   System.out.print(z);
   ```

   What is printed if x, y, and z are all equal to zero before the code segment executes?

   A. 0
   B. 1
   C. 2
   D. 4
   E. 6

3. Consider the following incomplete code segment:

```
int sum=0;
for ( int k=0; condition; k++ ) {
    statement1 ;
}
statement2;
```

Assume that variable A is an array of `ints`. Which of the following can be used to replace the placeholders *condition*, *statement1*, and *statement2* so that the code segment computes and returns the sum of the values in A?

	condition	statement1	statement2
A.	k < A.length	sum += A[k]	return sum
B.	k <= A.length	sum += A[k]	return sum
C.	k < A.length	sum++	System.out.println(sum)
D.	k <= A.length	sum++	return sum
E.	k <= A.length	sum += A[k]	System.out.println(sum)

4. The expression

```
(x && !y)
```

is equivalent to which of the following expressions?

A. `(x || !y)`

B. `(!x || y)`

C. `!(!x || y)`

D. `(!x && y)`

E. `!(!x && y)`

5. Which of the following best describes what a class's constructor should do?

A. Test all of the class's methods.

B. Initialize the fields of this instance of the class.

C. Determine and return the amount of storage needed by the fields of the class.

D. Return to free storage all memory used by this instance of the class.

E. Print a message informing the user that a new instance of this class has been created.

6. Consider the following three code segments, each of which is intended to define and initialize variable k:

Segment I	Segment II	Segment III
int k=10;	int	i
	k	n
	=	t
	10	k
	;	=
		10
		;

Which of the code segments will compile without error?

A. I only

B. I and II only

C. I and III only

D. II and III only

E. I, II, and III

7. Assume that variable A is an array of ints. Consider the following code segment:

```
// precondition: A.length > 0
   int x = 0;
   for (int k = 1; k < A.length; k++) {
       if (A[k] < A[x]) x = k;
   }
   return x;
```

Which of the following best describes what the code segment does?

A. It returns the value of the smallest element of A.

B. It returns the value of the largest element of A.

C. It returns the index of the smallest element of A.

D. It returns the index of the largest element of A.

E. It is not possible to determine what the code segment does without knowing how A is initialized.

Questions 8–10 rely on the following (incomplete) definition of the Book class:

```
public class Book {
    /*** fields ***/
    private double price;              // the price of this book

    /*** methods ***/
    public double getPrice() { ... } // returns the price of this
                                      // book

    public static double totalPrice( Book[] inventory ) {
    // postcondition: returns the sum of the prices of the books in
    //                  the inventory array
        double sum = 0.0;
        for (int k=0; k<inventory.length; k++) {
            // MISSING CODE
        }
        return sum;
    }
}
```

8. Consider adding a new method to the Book class that would permit the price of the book to be set when a variable of type Book was defined. For example:

    ```
    Book b1 = new Book(10.50);   // price of b1 is $10.50
    Book b2 = new Book(25.00);   // price of b2 is $25.00
    ```

    Which of the following best describes the new method that should be written?

    A. A constructor method with no arguments

    B. A constructor method with one argument

    C. A constructor method with two arguments

    D. A method named setPrice

    E. It is not possible to write a method that would work as specified

9. Which of the following code segments could be used to replace "// MISSING CODE" in method totalPrice so that it works as specified by its postcondition?

    A. sum += inventory.price[k];

    B. sum += inventory.getPrice(k);

    C. sum += inventory.Book[k];

    D. sum += inventory[k].Book();

    E. sum += inventory[k].getPrice();

10. Consider adding another method to the Book class with the following header:

```
public static double totalPrice( ArrayList inventory )
```

The new method would be the same as the existing totalPrice method except that its parameter, inventory, is an ArrayList of Books instead of an array of Books. Which of the following statements about the proposed new method is true?

A. It is an example of inheritance.

B. It is an example of an interface.

C. It is an example of overloading.

D. It is an example of an abstract method.

E. It is an example of casting.

11. Consider the following code segment:

```
for (int j=0; j<M; j++) {
    for (int k=0; k<N; k++) {
        System.out.print("*");
    }
    System.out.println();
}
```

Assume that M and N are int variables, initialized to 2 and 3, respectively. What is printed when the code segment executes?

A. ******

B. ***
    ***

C. **
    **
    **

D. *
    *

E. ******
    ******

Questions 12 and 13 rely on the following information:

A dairy farm has 100 cows, kept in 5 fields, with 20 cows per field. The farmer needs a data structure to record the amount of milk given by each cow in one day.

Two different data structures are being considered:

Structure 1:

An array of doubles of length 100. Each array entry is the amount of milk given by one cow on one day. The first 20 entries will be used for the cows in field 1, the next 20 entries will be used for the cows in field 2, and so on.

Structure 2:

Five arrays of doubles, each of length 20. Each array entry is the amount of milk given by one cow on one day. The first array will be used for the cows in field 1, the second array will be used for the cows in field 2, and so on.

12. The following operations are to be performed on the data structure:

Operation 1:

Compute, for each of the five fields, the total amount of milk produced by the cows in that field.

Operation 2:

Compute the total amount of milk produced by all of the cows.

Which of the following statements about these operations is true?

A. Both operations can be implemented using either of the two data structures.

B. Operation 1 can be implemented using either of the two data structures, but Operation 2 can only be implemented using Structure 1.

C. Operation 2 can be implemented using either of the two data structures, but Operation 1 can only be implemented using Structure 1.

D. Operation 1 can be implemented using either of the two data structures, but Operation 2 can only be implemented using Structure 2.

E. Operation 2 can be implemented using either of the two data structures, but Operation 1 can only be implemented using Structure 2.

13. Under which of the following conditions does Data Structure 1 require more storage than Data Structure 2?

    A. When the total amount of milk produced is the same for all five fields

    B. When the total amount of milk produced is different for each of the five fields

    C. When the cows in the first field produce the most milk, then the cows in the second field, then the cows in the third field, and so on.

    D. When the cows in the fifth field produce the most milk, then the cows in the fourth field, then the cows in the third field, and so on.

    E. Data Structure 1 never requires more storage than Data Structure 2.

14. Consider the following two code segments:

Segment 1	Segment 2

    ```
    Segment 1                       Segment 2

    while (k > 0) {                 while (k > 0) {
        System.out.println(k);         System.out.println(k);
        k--;                           k--;
    }                               }
                                    while (k > 0) {
                                        System.out.println(k);
                                        k--;
                                    }
    ```

    Assume that in both cases variable k has the *same* initial value. Under which of the following conditions will the two code segments produce identical output?

    I.   The initial value of k is greater than zero.
    II. The initial value of k is zero.
    III. The initial value of k is less than zero.

    A. I only

    B. II only

    C. III only

    D. I and III only

    E. I, II, and III

15. Assume that A and B are arrays of `ints`, both of the same length. Which of the following code segments returns `true` if and only if the two arrays contain the same sequence of values?

   A.   `return (A == B);`

   B.
```
for (int k=0; k < A.length; k++) {
    if (A[k] != B[k]) return false;
}
return true;
```

   C.   `return (A.equals(B));`

   D.
```
for (int k=0; k < A.length; k++) {
    if (A[k] == B[k]) return true;
}
return false;
```

   E.
```
boolean match;
for (int k=0; k < A.length; k++) {
    match = (A[k] == B[k]);
}
return match;
```

16. Assume that variable A is an ArrayList of size five. Consider the following code segment:

```
int N = A.size();
for (int k=0; k<=N/2; k++) {
    A.set(k, "X");
    A.set(N-k-1, "O");
}
```

Which of the following correctly illustrates A after the code segment executes?

   A. X X O O O

   B. X X X O O

   C. O O O O O

   D. X X X X

   E. It is not possible to determine the values in A after the code segment executes without knowing what values are in A before the code segment executes.

Questions 17 and 18 refer to the following information:

Assume that N and k are int variables and that A is an array of ints. Consider the following expression:

```
((k <= N) && (A[k] < 0)) || (A[k] == 0)
```

17. Under which of the following conditions must the expression evaluate to true?

    A. A[k] is not equal to zero.
    B. A[k] is equal to zero.
    C. k is less than N.
    D. k is less than or equal to N.
    E. k is less than N, and A[k] is not equal to zero.

18. Assume that A contains N+1 values. Recall that an out-of-bounds array index causes a runtime error. Which of the following statements is true?

    A. Evaluating the expression will never cause a runtime error.
    B. Evaluating the expression will cause a runtime error whenever A[k] is zero.
    C. Evaluating the expression will cause a runtime error whenever A[k] is not zero.
    D. Evaluating the expression will cause a runtime error whenever k is equal to N.
    E. Evaluating the expression will cause a runtime error whenever k is greater than N.

For questions 19–21, assume that variable A is an array of ints.

19. Consider the following code segment:

    ```
    for (int k=1; k<A.length; k++) {
        if (A[k-1] >= A[k]) return false;
    }
    return true;
    ```

    Which of the following best describes what the code segment does?

    A. Returns true if and only if array A contains duplicate values.
    B. Returns true if and only if array A contains at least one positive value.
    C. Returns true if and only if array A contains at least one negative value.
    D. Returns true if and only if array A is sorted in strictly ascending order.
    E. Returns true if and only if array A is sorted in strictly descending order.

20. Consider the following code segment:

```
boolean tmp=false;
for (int k=0; k<A.length; k++) {
    tmp = (A[k] == val);
}
return tmp;
```

Which of the following best characterizes the conditions under which this code segment returns `true`?

A. Whenever array A contains value `val`

B. Whenever the first element of array A has value `val`

C. Whenever the last element of array A has value `val`

D. Whenever more than one element of array A has value `val`

E. Whenever exactly one element of array A has value `val`

21. Consider the following incomplete code segment:

```
// postcondition:  returns true if some value occurs more than
//                  once in A; false otherwise
    for (int j=0; j<A.length-1; j++) {
        statement
    }
    return false;
```

Which of the following can be used to replace the placeholder *statement* so that the code segment works as specified by its postcondition?

A. `if (A[j] == A[j+1]) return true;`

B. `if (A[j] == A[A.length]) return true;`

C.
```
for (int k=0; k<A.length; k++) {
    if (A[j] == A[k]) return true;
}
```

D.
```
for (int k=j; k<A.length; k++) {
    if (A[j] == A[k]) return true;
}
```

E.
```
for (int k=j+1; k<A.length; k++) {
    if (A[j] == A[k]) return true;
}
```

22. Consider writing a program to be used to manage a collection of movies. There are three kinds of movies in the collection: dramas, comedies, and documentaries. The collector would like to keep track, for each movie, of its name, the name of the director, and the date when it was made. Some operations are to be implemented for all movies, and there will also be special operations for each of the three different kinds of movies. Which of the following is the best design?

A. Define one class, `Movie`, with six fields: `drama`, `comedy`, `documentary`, `name`, `director`, and `date`.

B. Define one superclass, `Movie`, with six subclasses: `Drama`, `Comedy`, `Documentary`, `Name`, `Director`, and `Date`.

C. Define one superclass, `Movie`, with three fields: `name`, `director`, and `date`; and with three subclasses: `Drama`, `Comedy`, and `Documentary`.

D. Define six unrelated classes: `Drama`, `Comedy`, `Documentary`, `Name`, `Director`, and `Date`.

E. Define six classes: `Drama`, `Comedy`, `Documentary`, `Name`, `Director`, and `Date`. Make `Date` and `Director` subclasses of `Name`, and make `Documentary` and `Comedy` subclasses of `Drama`.

23. Assume that a method called `checkStr` has been written to determine whether a string is the same forwards and backwards. The following two sets of data are being considered to be used to test method `checkStr`:

Data Set 1	Data Set 2
`"aba"`	`"abba"`
`"?"`	`"abab"`
`"z&*&z"`	
`"##"`	

Which of the following is an advantage of Data Set 2 over Data Set 1?

A. All strings in Data Set 2 have the same number of characters.

B. Data Set 2 contains a string for which method `checkStr` should return `false`, as well as a string for which method `checkStr` should return `true`.

C. The strings in Data Set 2 contain only lowercase letters.

D. Data Set 2 contains fewer values than Data Set 1.

E. Data Set 2 has no advantage over Data Set 1.

Questions 24 and 25 refer to the following recursive method:

```
public static int compute(int x, int y) {
    if (x == y) return x;
    else return( compute(x+1, y-1) );
}
```

24. What is returned by the call `compute(1, 5)`?

    A. 1

    B. 2

    C. 3

    D. 4

    E. No value is returned because an infinite recursion occurs.

25. Which of the following calls leads to an infinite recursion?

    I. `compute(2, 8)`
    II. `compute(8, 2)`
    III. `compute(2, 5)`

    A. I only

    B. II only

    C. III only

    D. I and II

    E. II and III

26. Consider the following code segment:

    ```
    String s1 = "ab";
    String s2 = s1;

    s1 = s1 + "c";
    System.out.println(s1 + " " + s2);
    ```

    What is printed when this code executes?

    A. abc ab

    B. abc abc

    C. ac ab

    D. ac ac

    E. ae ab

27. Assume that the following interface and class have been defined:

```
public interface Person {
    public String getName();
    public int getAge();
}

public class Student implements Person {
    /*** fields ***/
    private String name;
    private int age;

    /*** methods ***/
    public Student( String n, int a ) {    // constructor
        name = n;
        age = a;
    }
    public String getName() { return name; }
    public int getAge() { return age; }
}
```

Which of the following will cause a compile-time error?

A. An attempt to create an instance of a `Person`

B. An attempt to create an instance of a `Student`

C. An attempt to define a method with a parameter of type `Person`

D. An attempt to define a method with a parameter of type `Student`

E. An attempt to define a subclass of the `Student` class

28. Three algorithms are being considered to look for a given value in an *unsorted* array of integers.

   Algorithm 1: Use binary search.

   Algorithm 2: Use sequential search.

   Algorithm 3: Sort the array, then use binary search.

Which of the following statements about the three algorithms is true?

A. All three will work; Algorithm 1 will be most efficient.

B. Only Algorithms 1 and 2 will work; Algorithm 1 will be most efficient.

C. Only Algorithms 1 and 3 will work; Algorithm 1 will be most efficient.

D. Only Algorithms 2 and 3 will work; Algorithm 2 will be most efficient.

E. Only Algorithms 2 and 3 will work; Algorithm 3 will be most efficient.

29. Assume that variables s1 and s2 are both of type String. Consider the following three code segments:

Segment I	Segment II	Segment III
s1 = "hello";	s1 = "hello"	s1 = "hello"
s2 = s1;	s2 = "hello"	s2 = s1 + "!"

After executing which of the three segments will the expression s1 == s2 evaluate to true?

A. I only

B. II only

C. III only

D. I and II only

E. I, II, and III

30. Which of the following best explains why a method might have the precondition N > 0?

A. Every method must have a precondition or it will not compile.

B. Including a precondition makes a method more efficient.

C. Including the precondition ensures that if, when the method is called, variable N is *not* greater than 0, it will be set to 1 so that the precondition is satisfied.

D. Including the precondition provides information to users of the method, specifying what is expected to be true whenever the method is called.

E. This is an example of bottom-up design. The precondition is included to permit the method to be tested and debugged in isolation from the rest of the program. The precondition should be removed as soon as that phase of program development is complete.

Questions 31 and 32 concern the code segment shown below. The code segment was intended to count and return the number of values in *sorted* array A (which contains `int`s) that are smaller than the value in `int` variable x. However, the code segment sometimes causes a runtime error due to an out-of-bounds array index.

```
// precondition: A is sorted in ascending order.
   int k = 0;
   while ((A[k] < x) && (k < A.length)) k++;
   return k;
```

31. Under what conditions does the code segment cause an out-of-bounds array index?

   A. Always

   B. Whenever *no* values in array A are smaller than x

   C. Whenever *all* values in array A are smaller than x

   D. Whenever *some* value in array A is smaller than x

   E. Whenever *most* values in array A are smaller than x

32. Which of the following replacements for the `while-loop` condition would fix the code segment so that it works as intended?

   A. `(A[k] < x) || (k < A.length)`

   B. `(A[k] < x) && (k <= A.length)`

   C. `(A[k] <= x) && (k < A.length)`

   D. `(k < A.length) || (A[k] < x)`

   E. `(k < A.length) && (A[k] < x)`

33. Under which of the following conditions can a method be *overloaded*; that is, when can two methods with the same name be included in the same class?

   A. The methods do different things.

   B. The methods have different numbers or types of parameters.

   C. The methods have different parameter names.

   D. The methods have different preconditions.

   E. Two methods with the same name can never be included in the same class.

Questions 34 and 35 concern the following two ways to represent a set of integers (with no duplicates) with values in the range 0 to N:

Method 1:

Use an array of booleans of size $N + 1$. The kth element of the array is `true` if k is in the set; otherwise, it is `false`.

Method 2:

Use an array of integers. The size of the array is the same as the current size of the set. Each element of the array holds one of the values that is in the set. The values are stored in the array in sorted order.

34. Which of the following statements about the storage requirements of the two methods is true?

A. Method 1 requires less storage than Method 2 to represent an empty set.

B. The amount of storage required for Method 1 is independent of the number of values in the set, whereas the amount of storage required for Method 2 varies depending on the number of values in the set.

C. The amount of storage required for Method 2 is independent of the number of values in the set, whereas the amount of storage required for Method 1 varies depending on the number of values in the set.

D. The amount of storage required for both Method 1 and Method 2 is independent of the number of values in the set.

E. The amount of storage required for both Method 1 and Method 2 varies depending on the number of values in the set.

35. Which of the following operations can be implemented more efficiently using Method 1 rather than using Method 2?

    I. Determine whether a given value is in the set.
    II. Remove a given value from the set.
    III. Print all of the values in the set.

A. I only

B. II only

C. III only

D. I and II only

E. I, II, and III

36. Two programmers are working together to write a program. One is implementing a `List` class, and the other is writing code that includes variables of type `List`. The programmers have decided that the `List` class will include a public method named `search`. Which of the following facts about the `search` method does *not* need to be agreed on by both programmers?

    A. The names of the parameters
    B. The number of parameters
    C. The pre- and postconditions
    D. The type of each parameter
    E. The return type

37. Assume that variable `L` is an ArrayList that contains a sequence of `Integers`. Consider the following (incomplete) code segment:

    ```
    int sum = 0;
    for (int k=0; k<L.size(); k++) {
        sum += expression;
    }
    ```

    Which of the following could be used to replace *expression* so that the code segment correctly computes the sum of the values in the list?

    A. `L.get(k)`
    B. `((Integer)(L.get(k))).intValue()`
    C. `(int)(L.get(k))`
    D. `(Integer)(L.get(k))`
    E. `((int)(L.get(k))).intValue()`

38. Consider the following recursive method. (Assume that method `readInt` reads one integer value typed in by the user.)

```java
public static void print(int n) {
    int x;
    if (n > 0) {
        x = readInt();
        if (x > 0) {
            print(n-1);
            System.out.println(x);
        }
        else print(n);
    }
}
```

Which of the following best describes what happens as a result of the call `print(5)`?

A. The first five numbers typed by the user are printed in the order in which they are typed.

B. The first five numbers typed by the user are printed in the opposite order to that in which they are typed.

C. The first five positive numbers typed by the user are printed in the order in which they are typed.

D. The first five positive numbers typed by the user are printed in the opposite order to that in which they are typed.

E. Nothing is printed because the call causes an infinite recursion.

39. Assume that arrays A and B both contain `int` values. Which of the following code segments returns `true` if and only if the kth elements of the two arrays are the same?

```
I.   return(A[k] == B[k]);
II.  if (A[k] == B[k]) {
         return true;
     }
     else return false;
III. if (A[k] == B[k]) {
         return true;
     }
     return false;
```

A. I only

B. II only

C. III only

D. II and III only

E. I, II, and III

40. Consider the following code segment:

```
x = y;
y = !x;
x = !y;
```

Assume that x and y are initialized boolean variables. Which of the following statements is true?

A. The final value of x is the same as the initial value of x.

B. The final value of x is the same as the initial value of y.

C. The final value of y is the same as the initial value of y.

D. The final value of y is the same as the initial value of x.

E. It is not possible to say anything about the final values of x and y without knowing their initial values.

A Practice Examination 2

Section II

Time — 1 hour and 45 minutes
Number of questions — 4
Percent of total grade — 50

Question 1

Part (a)

Write method `numInArray`, as started below. `numInArray` should return the number of times the string `s` occurs in array `A`.

For example, assume that array `A` is as shown below.

```
    [0]      [1]     [2]      [3]     [4]      [5]     [6]
  "java"    "is"   "nice"    "so"   "nice"    "it"    "is"
```

Here are some examples of calls to method `numInArray`:

Method call	Returned value
numInArray(A, "java")	1
numInArray(A, "is")	2
numInArray(A, "nice")	2
numInArray(A, "ja")	0

Complete method `numInArray` below.

```
public static int numInArray(String[] A, String s) {
// postcondition: returns the number of times s occurs in A
```

Part (b)

Write method `printAllNums`, as started below. For every string s in array A, `printAllNums` should write (using `System.out.println`) the string s, followed by a colon and a space, then followed by the number of times that string occurs in array B.

For example, assume that arrays A and B are as shown below.

```
            [0]      [1]       [2]      [3]
   A:       "ice"    "cream"   "is"     "nice"

            [0]      [1]      [2]      [3]     [4]      [5]     [6]
   B:       "java"   "is"     "nice"   "so"    "nice"   "it"    "is"
```

The call `printAllNums(A, B)` should produce the following output:

```
ice: 0
cream: 0
is: 2
nice: 2
```

In writing `printAllNums`, you may include calls to method `numInArray` specified above in Part (a). Assume that `numInArray` works as specified, regardless of what you wrote in Part (a).

Complete method `printAllNums` below.

```
public static void printAllNums( String[] A, String[] B ) {
// postcondition: for all k such that 0 <= k < A.length,
//                prints the string in A[k] followed by a colon
//                and a space and the number of times that string
//                occurs in B
```

Question 2

This question concerns the Money class, partially defined below.

```
public class Money {
    /*** fields ***/
    private double amount;

    /*** public methods ***/
    public String toString( ) {
        ...
    }

    /*** private methods ***/
    private int getDollars( ) {
    // postcondition: returns the whole-number part of the value in
    //                 the amount field
        ...
    }

    private int getCents( ) {
    // postcondition: returns the fractional part of the value in
    //                 the amount field as an int in the range 0 to 99
        ...
    }
}
```

Part (a)

Write the getDollars method of the Money class. Method getDollars returns the whole-number part of the value in the amount field (as an int). For example:

amount	Value returned by getDollars( )
123.40	123
0.33	0
10.00	10
0.00	0

Complete method getDollars below.

```
public int getDollars( ) {
    // postcondition: returns the whole-number part of the value in
    //                 the amount field
```

Part (b)

Write the getCents method of the Money class. Method getCents returns the fractional part of the value in the amount field as an int in the range 0 to 99. For example:

amount	Value returned by getCents( )
123.40	40
12.04	4
0.33	33
45.00	0

Remember that decimal numbers cannot always be represented exactly by a computer. For example, the number 12.04 might be represented as 12.03999999999999915. This means that your getCents method will need to do some rounding in order to compute correct values in all cases.

Complete method getCents below. In writing method getCents, you may include calls to method getDollars specified in Part (a). Assume that method getDollars works as specified, regardless of what you wrote for Part (a).

```
public int getCents( ) {
    // postcondition: returns the fractional part of the value in the
    //                 amount field as an int in the range 0 to 99
```

Part (c)

Write the `toString` method of the `Money` class. Method `toString` should print the amount of money in the form:

xx dollars and yy cents

where *xx* is the whole-number part of the value in the `amount` field, and *yy* is the fractional part of the value in the `amount` field.

For example:

amount	Value returned by `toString(S)`
123.40	123 dollars and 40 cents
12.04	12 dollars and 4 cents
0.33	0 dollars and 33 cents
45.00	45 dollars and 0 cents

In writing method `toString`, you may include calls to method `getDollars` specified in Part (a) and method `getCents` specified in Part (b). Assume that those two methods work as specified, regardless of what you wrote for Parts (a) and (b).

Complete method `toString` below.

```
public String toString( ) {
```

Question 3

This question involves the following two (incomplete) class definitions, which define classes to be used for storing information about the students in an AP CS class.

```
public class APCS {
    /*** fields ***/
    private StudentInfo[] students;
    private String highestAverage;

    /*** constructor ***/
    public APCS() {
        ...
    }
}

public class StudentInfo {
    /*** fields ***/
    private String name;
    private int[] grades;
    private double averageGrade;

    /*** methods ***/
    // constructor
    public StudentInfo( String theName, int[] theGrades ) {
        ...
    }

    public String getName() { return name; }
    public double getAverageGrade() { return averageGrade; }
}
```

Part (a)

Write the constructor for the StudentInfo class. The constructor should initialize the name and grades fields using the given values, and then it should compute the average grade and use that value to initialize the averageGrade field. (If the number of grades is zero, the averageGrade field should be set to zero.)

Complete the constructor below.

```
public StudentInfo( String theName, int[] theGrades ) {
```

Part (b)

Assume that the following methods can be used to read input values from a file.

```
public static int readInt()      \\ reads and returns the next
                                 \\ integer value
public static String readString()  \\ reads and returns the next
                                   \\ string value
```

Write the constructor for the APCS class. Assume that when the constructor is called, there is an input file ready for reading. The first piece of data in the file is a positive integer N, the number of students in the class. Then there is information for each of the N students, organized as follows:

The student's name

The number of grades recorded for that student

The actual grades (integers in the range 0 to 100)

The APCS constructor should initialize its students field by creating an array of StudentInfo, using the data in the input file. It should then determine which student has the highest average and use that student's name to initialize its highestAverage field. (If two students share the same, highest average, either name can be used to initialize the highestAverage field.)

For example, if the input data are as follows:

```
2
Jones
5
100 95 80 100 100
Smith
2
86 87
```

the students field should be initialized to contain two StudentInfo elements (one for Jones and one for Smith), and the highestAverage field should be initialized to "Jones", because Jones has an average grade of 95.0, whereas Smith has a (lower) average grade of 86.5.

In writing the APCS constructor, you may include calls to the StudentInfo constructor, specified above in Part (a). Assume that the StudentInfo constructor works as specified, regardless of what you wrote for Part (a).

Complete the APCS constructor below.

```
public APCS() {
```

Question 4

Assume that a class called `BankAccount` has been implemented to represent one person's bank account and that the `BankAccount` class includes the following public methods:

```
public int getAccountNum()              // returns the account
                                        // number
public double getBalance()              // returns the current
                                        // balance (how much
                                        // money is currently
                                        // in the account)
public void doDeposit(double amount)    // adds amount to the
                                        // current balance
public void doWithdrawal(double amount) // subtracts amount from
                                        // the current balance
```

Also assume that a class called `Transaction` has been defined to represent information about one transaction on a bank account (one deposit or one withdrawal), including the following public methods:

```
public int getAccountNum()         // returns account number
public String getTransactionType() // returns "d" for deposit,
                                   // "w" for withdrawal
public double getAmount()          // returns the amount to be
                                   // deposited or withdrawn
```

For this question, you will write the methods of the Bank class, outlined below:

```
import ap.java.util.ArrayList;

public class Bank {
    /*** fields ***/
    private BankAccount[] accounts;

    /*** public methods ***/
    public void oneTransaction(Transaction trans) {
    // precondition: no two BankAccounts in the accounts array
    //               have the same account number;
    //               one of the BankAccounts in the accounts array
    //               has account number trans.getAccountNum();
    //               trans.getTransactionType() is either "d" or "w"
        ...
    }
```

```
public ArrayList daysTransactions(Transaction[] transactions) {
// precondition:  no two BankAccounts in the accounts array
//                have the same account number;
//                for every transaction in the transactions
//                array, there is a BankAccount in the accounts
//                array with the same account number;
//                for every transaction in the transactions
//                array, the transaction type is either "d"
//                or "w"
    ...
}


/*** private methods ***/
private int findAccount( int accountNum ) {
// precondition: no two BankAccounts in the accounts array
//               have the same account number
// postcondition: returns the index of the BankAccount in the
//                accounts array with the given account number,
//                or -1 if there is no such BankAccount in the
//                array
    ...
}
}
```

Part (a)

Write the findAccount method of the Bank class. Method findAccount should return the index of the BankAccount in the accounts array with the given account number, or -1 if there is no such BankAccount in the array.

Complete method findAccount below.

```
public int findAccount( int accountNum )
// precondition: no two BankAccounts in the accounts array have
//               the same account number
// postcondition: returns the index of the BankAccount in the
//                accounts array with the given account number, or
//                -1 if there is no such BankAccount in the array
```

Part (b)

Write the oneTransaction method of the Bank class. Method oneTransaction has one parameter: a Transaction. Method oneTransaction should find the BankAccount with the account number in the given Transaction, and it should deposit or withdraw the amount in the given Transaction from that account as appropriate.

For example, assume that accounts.length is 4 and that the elements in the array have the account numbers and balances shown below.

	[0]	[1]	[2]	[3]
account #:	100	107	102	105
balance:	100.27	57.30	150.00	5.25

Here are some examples to illustrate what the call oneTransaction(trans) should do:

Value of trans		Modified element of accounts array
accountNum:	107	[1]
transactionType:	"d"	107
amount:	10.50	67.80
accountNum:	100	[0]
transactionType:	"w"	100
amount:	100.27	0.0
accountNum:	105	[3]
transactionType:	"w"	105
amount:	6.00	-.75

In writing method oneTransaction, you may include calls to method findAccount, specified above in Part (a). Assume that findAccount works as specified, regardless of what you wrote for Part (a).

Complete method oneTransaction below.

```
public void oneTransaction(Transaction trans) {
// precondition: no two BankAccounts in the accounts array
//               have the same account number;
//               one of the BankAccounts in the accounts array
//               has account number trans.getAccountNum();
//               trans.getTransactionType() is either "d" or "w"
```

Part (c)

Write the `daysTransactions` method of the `Bank` class.   Method `daysTransactions` has one parameter: an array of `Transactions` named `transactions`. Method `daysTransactions` should carry out each of the transactions in the `transactions` array. It should also create and return an `ArrayList` containing all of the `BankAccounts` in the `accounts` array that are overdrawn (have a negative balance) at the end of the day (either because they were overdrawn initially and the transactions did not correct that situation, or because carrying out the transactions left them overdrawn).

For example, if the `accounts` array is initially as shown above in Part (b), and if the `transactions` array contains all three of the example transactions shown in Part (b), then the returned `ArrayList` should contain just one element, the `BankAccount` with account number 105, because that is the only account with a negative balance after the three transactions have been performed.

In writing method `daysTransactions`, you may include calls to method `findAccount`, specified above in Part (a), and/or `oneTransaction`, specified above in Part (b). Assume that `findAccount` and `oneTransaction` work correctly, regardless of what you wrote for Parts (a) and (b).

Complete method `daysTransactions` below.

```
public ArrayList daysTransactions(Transaction[] transactions) {
// precondition:  no two BankAccounts in the accounts array
//                have the same account number;
//                for every transaction in the transactions array,
//                there is a BankAccount in the accounts array
//                with the same account number;
//                for every transaction in the transactions array,
//                the transaction type is either "d" or "w"
```

Answers to A Practice Examination 2

Section I

1.	D	21.	E
2.	A	22.	C
3.	A	23.	B
4.	C	24.	C
5.	B	25.	E
6.	B	26.	A
7.	C	27.	A
8.	B	28.	D
9.	E	29.	A
10.	C	30.	D
11.	B	31.	C
12.	A	32.	E
13.	E	33.	B
14.	E	34.	B
15.	B	35.	D
16.	A	36.	A
17.	B	37.	B
18.	E	38.	D
19.	D	39.	E
20.	C	40.	B

Answers to A Practice Examination 2

Section II

Question 1

Part (a)

```
public static int numInArray(String[] A, String s) {
// postcondition: returns the number of times s occurs in A
int count = 0;

    for (int k=0; k<A.length; k++) {
        if (A[k].equals(s)) count++;
    }
    return count;
}
```

Common errors:

- Using == instead of `equals`
- Forgetting to initialize `count`
- Forgetting to return `count`

Part (b)

```
public static void printAllNums( String[] A, String[] B ) {
// postcondition: for all k such that 0 <= k < A.length,
//                prints the string in A[k] followed by a colon
//                and a space and the number of times that string
//                occurs in B
    for (int k=0; k<A.length; k++) {
        System.out.println(A[k] + ": " + numInArray(B, A[k]));
    }
}
```

Question 2

Part (a)

```
private int getDollars( ) {
// postcondition: returns the whole-number part of the value in the
//                amount field
    return (int)amount;
}
```

Part (b)

Version 1

Subtract the whole-number part of amount, then multiply by 100, add .5, and truncate using a cast.

```
private int getCents( ) {
// postcondition: returns the fractional part of the value in the
//                amount field as an int in the range 0 to 99
    int dollars = getDollars();
    double cents = (amount - dollars) * 100 + .5;
    return (int)cents;
}
```

Version 2

Multiply by 100, add .5, and truncate using a cast, then get just the cents part using the modulus operator.

```
private int getCents( ) {
// postcondition: returns the fractional part of the value in the
//                amount field as an int in the range 0 to 99
        int cents = (int)(amount * 100 + .5);
        return cents % 100;
}
```

Version 3

Remove the whole-number part using the modulus operator, then multiply by 100, add .5, and truncate using a cast.

```
private int getCents( ) {
// postcondition: returns the fractional part of the value in the
//                  amount field as an int in the range 0 to 99
    double cents = amount % 1;
    return (int) (cents * 100 + .5);
}
```

Part (c)

```
public String toString( ) {
    return ( getDollars() + " dollars and " + getCents() + " cents " );
}
```

Question 3

Part (a)

```
public StudentInfo( String theName, int[] theGrades ) {
    int sum = 0;

    name = theName;
    grades = theGrades;
    for (int k=0; k<grades.length; k++) {
        sum += grades[k];
    }
    if (grades.length > 0) {
        averageGrade = ((double)sum)/grades.length;
    }
    else averageGrade = 0;
}
```

Common errors:

- Forgetting to test whether the number of grades is zero
- Getting a truncated value for the average (because both the numerator and the denominator are `int`s, and no cast is used)

Part (b)

```
public APCS() {

    // initialize students array
    int numStudents = readInt();
    students = new StudentInfo[numStudents];
    for (int k=0; k<numStudents; k++) {
        String name = readString();
        int numGrades = readInt();
        int[] grades = new int[numGrades];
        for (int j=0; j<numGrades; j++) {
            grades[j] = readInt();
        }
        students[k] = new StudentInfo(name, grades);
    }

    // initialize highestAverage field
    double max = students[0].getAverageGrade();
    highestAverage = students[0].getName();
    for (int k=1; k<numStudents; k++) {
        double oneAv = students[k].getAverageGrade();
        if (oneAv > max) highestAverage = students[k].getName();
    }
}
```

Question 4

Part (a)

```java
private int findAccount( int accountNum ) {
// precondition: no two BankAccounts in the accounts array have the
//               same account number
// postcondition: returns the index of the BankAccount in the
//                accounts array with the given account number, or
//                -1 if there is no such BankAccount in the array
    for (int k=0; k<accounts.length; k++) {
        if (accounts[k].getAccountNum() == accountNum) return k;
    }
    return -1;
}
```

Part (b)

```java
public void oneTransaction(Transaction trans) {
// precondition: no two BankAccounts in the accounts array
//               have the same account number;
//               one of the BankAccounts in the accounts array
//               has account number trans.getAccountNum();
//               trans.getTransactionType() is either "d" or "w"
    int k = findAccount(trans.getAccountNum());
    if (trans.getTransactionType().equals("d")) {
        accounts[k].doDeposit(trans.getAmount());
    }
    else {
        accounts[k].doWithdrawal(trans.getAmount());
    }
}
```

Part (c)

```
public ArrayList daysTransactions(Transaction[] transactions) {
// precondition:  no two BankAccounts in the accounts array
//                have the same account number;
//                for every transaction in the transactions array,
//                there is a BankAccount in the accounts array
//                with the same account number;
//                for every transaction in the transactions array,
//                the transaction type is either "d" or "w"
    ArrayList A = new ArrayList();
    for (int k=0; k<transactions.length; k++) {
        oneTransaction(transactions[k]);
    }
    for (int k=0; k<accounts.length; k++) {
        if (accounts[k].getBalance() < 0) A.add(accounts[k]);
    }
    return A;
}
```

Common errors:

- Putting an account number into the `ArrayList` immediately after processing a withdrawal transaction that makes that account's balance negative (this is an error because (a) it misses accounts that started out overdrawn and were not affected by the transactions, and (b) it erroneously includes accounts that temporarily became overdrawn but were fixed up by a later deposit).

- Confusion about indexing (e.g., passing the entire `transactions` array to method `oneTransaction`)

- Trying to access the fields of the `BankAccount` and/or `Transaction` class directly rather than by using their public methods

AB Practice Examination 1

Section I

Time — 1 hour and 15 minutes
Number of questions — 40
Percent of total grade — 50

1. Assume that variable L points to the first node of a nonempty, singly linked list of integers. Which of the following operations can be performed in constant ($O(1)$) time?

    A. Add a node at the front of the list.

    B. Add a node at the end of the list.

    C. Add a node in the middle of the list.

    D. Determine how many nodes are in the list.

    E. Compute the sum of all values in the list.

2. For which of the following trees do a preorder and an inorder traversal produce the same sequence of letters?

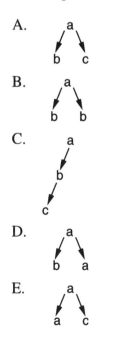

A.

B.

C.

D.

E.

3. Assume that `val` is an `int` variable initialized to be greater than zero and that `A` is an array of `int`s. Consider the following code segment:

```
for (int k=0; k<A.length; k++) {
    while (A[k] < val) {
        A[k] *= 2;
    }
}
```

Which of the following best describes when this code segment will go into an infinite loop?

A. Always

B. Whenever `A` includes a value greater than `val`

C. Whenever `A` includes a value less than `val`

D. Whenever `A` includes a value equal to `val`

E. Whenever `A` includes a value less than or equal to zero

4. Which of the following is a valid reason for using a doubly linked list rather than a singly linked list?

A. Less storage is required for a doubly linked list than for a singly linked list.

B. A doubly linked list can be used to implement a stack, whereas a singly linked list cannot.

C. The number of items in the list can be determined more efficiently using a doubly linked list than using a singly linked list.

D. Given a pointer to a node n in the middle of the list, the node before n can be removed more efficiently using a doubly linked list than using a singly linked list.

E. Given a pointer to a node n in the middle of the list, a new node can be inserted immediately after n more efficiently using a doubly linked list than using a singly linked list.

5. Which of the following is a property of all binary search trees?

A. For all nodes n, the number of nodes in n's left subtree is the same as the number of nodes in n's right subtree.

B. The number of leaves is the same as the number of nonleaves.

C. The time required to search for a given value is proportional to the height of the tree (the longest path from the root to a leaf) in the worst case.

D. Every node has either 0 or 2 children.

E. The time required to insert a new value into a tree with N nodes is $O(N^2)$ in the worst case.

6. Consider the following code segment:

    ```
    x = (x || y);
    y = (x && y);
    ```

    Assume that x and y are initialized boolean variables. Which of the following statements is true?

    A. The final value of x is the same as the initial value of x.

    B. The final value of x is the same as the initial value of y.

    C. The final value of y is the same as the initial value of y.

    D. The final value of y is the same as the initial value of x.

    E. It is not possible to say anything about the final values of x and y without knowing their initial values.

Questions 7 and 8 concern the design of a data structure to store information about which seats in a theater are reserved. The theater has ten rows; each row has 50 seats. Two data structures are being considered:

Data Structure 1:

> A two-dimensional array of booleans. The rows of the array correspond to the rows in the theater, and the columns of the array correspond to the seats in each row. An array element is `true` if and only if the corresponding seat is reserved.

Data Structure 2:

> A linked list of `Reservations`. Each `Reservation` has two integer fields: a row number and a seat number. The list is initially empty. Each time a seat is reserved, a new node is added to the front of the list, containing the row and seat numbers of the newly reserved seat.

7. Assume that the same amount of storage is required for an integer and a boolean. Under which of the following conditions does Data Structure 1 require less storage than Data Structure 2?

    A. No seats are reserved.

    B. All seats are reserved.

    C. Only a single seat in the first row is reserved.

    D. Only a single seat in the last row is reserved.

    E. Data Structure 1 never requires less storage than Data Structure 2.

8. Which of the following operations can be implemented more efficiently using Data Structure 1 than using Data Structure 2?

    Operation I:

    Determine how many seats are reserved.

    Operation II:

    Determine whether a particular seat (given its row and seat number) is reserved.

    Operation III:

    Determine whether the seats on either side of a particular seat (given its row and seat numbers) are both reserved.

    A. I only
    B. II only
    C. III only
    D. I and II
    E. II and III

9. Consider writing a program to be used by a company that sells cars. Four kinds of cars are sold: compact cars, station wagons, convertibles, and sedans. Assume that a `Car` class has been defined. Which of the following is the best way to represent the four different kinds of cars?

    A. The four kinds of cars should be represented using one field of the `Car` class: an array of four strings.

    B. The four kinds of cars should be represented as four `int` fields of the `Car` class, with one field for each kind of car.

    C. The four kinds of cars should be represented as four subclasses of the `Car` class.

    D. The four kinds of cars should be represented as four new classes, unrelated to the `Car` class.

    E. The four kinds of cars should be represented as four new classes. The `CompactCar` class should be a subclass of the `Car` class; the `StationWagon` class should be a subclass of the `CompactCar` class; the `Convertible` class should be a subclass of the `StationWagon` class; and the `Sedan` class should be a subclass of the `Convertible` class.

10. The code segment shown below was intended to set all of the elements on the diagonals of array A (an array of `int`s) to 0 and to set the element in the middle of the array to 1. However, the code segment does not work as intended. (Line numbers are included for reference.)

```
1. // precondition:  A is a nonempty, square array with
2. //                  an odd number of rows and columns
3.     int size = A.length;
4.     A[size/2][size/2] = 1;
5.     for (int j=0; j<size; j++) A[j][j] = 0;
6.     for (int j=0; j<size; j++) A[j][size-j-1] = 0;
```

When the code segment is tested, it is discovered that although the diagonal elements are set to 0, the middle element is also set to 0 instead of to 1. Which of the following changes fixes the code segment?

A. Change line 3 to `int size = A.length-1;`.

B. Change line 4 to `A[size/2+1][size/2+1] = 1;`.

C. Swap lines 4 and 5.

D. Swap lines 4 and 6.

E. Swap lines 5 and 6.

Questions 11 and 12 concern the following definition of class `List`, intended to be used to represent a list of objects (note that the `List` class uses the standard `ListNode` class).

```
public class List {
    /*** fields ***/
    private ListNode first;    // pointer to the first node
                               // in the list
    private ListNode last;     // pointer to the last node
                               // in the list

    /** methods **/
    public List( ) {first = last = null; }   // constructor

    public void addToEnd(Object ob) {
        ListNode tmp = new ListNode(ob, null);
        if (last != null) last.setNext(tmp);
        last = tmp;
    }
}
```

An empty list is intended to be represented by a `List` in which `first` and `last` are both `null`. A nonempty list is intended to be represented by a `List` in which:

• The items in the list are stored in a linked list.

• `first` points to the first node in the linked list.

• `last` points to the last node in the linked list.

However, the `List` class has not been implemented correctly.

11.   What is the problem with the implementation of the `List` class?

   A.   The constructor is not implemented correctly.

   B.   The types of the `first` and `last` fields are wrong.

   C.   The `addToEnd` method will not work correctly when the first value is added to the list.

   D.   The `addToEnd` method will not work correctly when a value other than the first is added to the list.

   E.   The `addToEnd` method will not work correctly when a duplicate value is added to the list.

12.   Which of the following best characterizes the running time of the version of `addToEnd` given above for a list that initially contains *n* values?

   A. $O(1)$

   B. $O(\log n)$

   C. $O(n)$

   D. $O(n \log n)$

   E. $O(n^2)$

13.   Consider adding the following recursive method to the standard `TreeNode` class:

```
public int mystery( ) {
    if (left == null && right == null) return 1;
    if (left == null) return (1 + right.mystery());
    if (right == null) return (1 + left.mystery());
    return(1 + left.mystery() + right.mystery());
}
```

   Which of the following best describes what method `mystery` does?

   A.   Always returns 0

   B.   Returns the number of nodes in the tree

   C.   Returns the number of leaves in the tree

   D.   Returns the number of nonleaves in the tree

   E.   Returns the height of the tree

14. A card game is played by two people as follows:

    - Initially, each person has half of the cards, placed face-down in a pile.
    - Repeat until at least one person has no more cards:
        Each person turns over the top card of his or her pile.
        If the cards are the same, they are both discarded.
        Otherwise, the person with the higher card takes both cards and puts them face-down on the bottom of his or her pile.

    Which of the following would be the most appropriate data structure(s) to use in a program that simulates this card game?

    A. A single stack

    B. A single queue

    C. Two stacks, one for each person

    D. Two queues, one for each person

    E. A stack for one person and a queue for the other person

15. Consider writing a program to be used to manage information about the animals on a farm. The farm has three kinds of animals: cows, pigs, and goats. The cows are used to produce both milk and meat. The goats are used only to produce milk, and the pigs are used only to produce meat.

    Assume that an `Animal` class has been defined. Which of the following is the best way to represent the remaining data?

    A. Define two subclasses of the `Animal` class: `MilkProducer` and `MeatProducer`. Define two subclasses of the `MilkProducer` class: `Cow` and `Goat`; and define two subclasses of the `MeatProducer` class: `Cow` and `Pig`.

    B. Define three subclasses of the `Animal` class: `Cow`, `Goat`, and `Pig`. Also define two interfaces: `MilkProducer` and `MeatProducer`. Define the `Cow` and `Goat` classes to implement the `MilkProducer` interface, and define the `Cow` and `Pig` classes to implement the `MeatProducer` interface.

    C. Define five new classes, not related to the `Animal` class: `Cow`, `Goat`, `Pig`, `MilkProducer`, and `MeatProducer`.

    D. Define five subclasses of the `Animal` class: `Cow`, `Goat`, `Pig`, `MilkProducer`, and `MeatProducer`.

    E. Define two subclasses of the `Animal` class: `MilkProducer` and `MeatProducer`. Also define three interfaces: `Cow`, `Goat`, and `Pig`. Define the `MilkProducer` class to implement the `Cow` and `Goat` interfaces, and define the `MeatProducer` class to implement the `Cow` and `Pig` interfaces.

For questions 16 and 17, assume that binary trees are implemented using the standard `TreeNode` class. Consider adding the following (incomplete) method to that class:

```
public void traverseTree(some-type X) {
    X.add-op( value );
    if (left != null) left.traverseTree(X);
    X.remove-op();
    X.add-op( value );
    if (right != null) right.traverseTree(X);
}
```

Assume that variable `T` is a `TreeNode`, initialized as shown below.

16. Assume that *some-type* is a stack of `Integers` and that *add-op* and *remove-op* are `push` and `pop`, respectively.

    Also, assume that variable `X` is an empty stack of `Integers`.

    Which of the following correctly describes what happens as the result of the call `T.traverseTree(X)`?

    A. A runtime error occurs when processing the root node of the tree due to an attempt to pop an empty stack.

    B. A runtime error occurs when processing a leaf node of the tree due to an attempt to pop an empty stack.

    C. The program executes without error; the final value of stack X is 1 2 3 (with 1 at the top).

    D. The program executes without error; the final value of stack X is 1 3 3 (with 1 at the top).

    E. The program executes without error; the final value of stack X is 3 1 1 (with 3 at the top).

17. Assume that *some-type* is a queue of `Integers` and that *add-op* and *remove-op* are enqueue and dequeue, respectively. Also, assume that variable `X` is an empty queue of `Integers`.

    Which of the following correctly describes what happens as the result of the call `T.traverseTree(X)`?

    A. A runtime error occurs when processing the root node of the tree due to an attempt to dequeue from an empty queue.

    B. A runtime error occurs when processing a leaf node of the tree due to an attempt to dequeue from an empty queue.

    C. The program executes without error; the final value of queue `X` is 1 2 3 (with 1 at the front of the queue).

    D. The program executes without error; the final value of queue `X` is 1 3 3 (with 1 at the front of the queue).

    E. The program executes without error; the final value of queue `X` is 3 1 1 (with 3 at the front of the queue).

18. Assume that `A` is an array of `ints` and that `val` is an `int`. Consider the following code segment:

    ```
    boolean tmp = false;
    for (int k=0; k<A.length; k++) {
        if (!tmp) tmp = (A[k] == val);
    }
    return tmp;
    ```

    Which of the following best characterizes the conditions under which this code segment returns `true`?

    A. Whenever array `A` contains value `val`

    B. Whenever the first element of array `A` has value `val`

    C. Whenever the last element of array `A` has value `val`

    D. Whenever more than one element of array `A` have value `val`

    E. Whenever exactly one element of array `A` has value `val`

19. Assume that A is a nonempty, rectangular, two-dimensional array of `ints`. Consider the following method:

```
for (int j=0; j<A[0].length; j++) {
    if (A[0][j] != A[A.length-1][j]) return false;
}
return true;
}
```

Which of the following best characterizes the conditions under which this code segment returns `true`?

A. Whenever the first and last rows of array A contain the same values

B. Whenever the first and second rows of array A contain the same values

C. Whenever the first and last columns of array A contain the same values

D. Whenever the first row and the first column of array A contain the same values

E. Whenever the first row and the last column of array A contain the same values

20. Which of the following best defines what it means to have a *collision* in a hashtable?

A. The hashtable becomes full.

B. The hash function returns a negative value.

C. Two different values that hash to the same location are inserted into the hashtable.

D. The hash function returns a value that is greater than the size of the hashtable.

E. The hash function is called more than once with the same value, so it returns the same result multiple times.

Questions 21 and 22 concern the `SortedList` class, a class for storing a list of `Comparable` objects in ascending order. A partial class definition is given below.

```
public class SortedList {
    /*** fields ***
    private int numVals;        // the number of values in the list
    private type vals;          // the values in the list,
                                // stored in ascending order

    /*** methods ***/
    public SortedList() ...         // constructor
    public void add(Comparable x) ...// adds x to the sorted list
    public Comparable get(int k) ... // returns the kth value in the
                                    // list (counting from 0)
    public int length() ...         // returns the number of values
                                    // in the list

}
```

21. Consider two ways to implement the `SortedList` class:

Implementation I:

The values are stored *in ascending order* in an array (i.e., *type* is `Comparable[]`). The array is initially of size 10. Whenever the array becomes full, a new array of twice the size is created, and the values are copied from the old array to the new array.

Implementation II:

The values are stored *in ascending order* in a linked list using the standard `ListNode` class to represent each node in the list (i.e., *type* is `ListNode`, and `vals` is a pointer to the first node in the linked list).

Which of the `SortedList` methods can be implemented more efficiently (in terms of Big-O notation) using an array rather than a linked list?

A.   Method `add` only

B.   Method `get` only

C.   Methods `add` and `get` only

D.   Methods `add` and `length` only

E.   Methods `add`, `get`, and `length`

22. Consider writing a private `SortedList` method to help test whether the `SortedList` class has been implemented correctly. An incomplete version of the method is given below.

```
private void test( ) {
    for (int k=0; k<length()-1; k++) {
        if (condition) {
            System.out.println (
                    "error:  list not sorted in ascending order");
        }
    }
}
```

Which of the following would be the best replacement for the placeholder *condition*?

A. `length() != k`

B. `length() > k`

C. `add(k)`

D. `get(k).compareTo(get(k+1)) > 0`

E. `!get(k).equals(get(k+1))`

Questions 23 and 24 concern the following information:

Assume that binary trees are implemented using the standard TreeNode class. Consider adding the following methods to the TreeNode class:

```
private static int max(Comparable x, Comparable y) {
    if (x.compareTo(y) > 0) return x;
    else return y;
}

public Comparable treeComp() {
    if (left == null && right == null) {
        return((Comparable)value);
    }
    if (left == null) {
        return(max((Comparable)value, right.treeComp()));
    }
    if (right == null) {
        return(max((Comparable)value, left.treeComp()));
    }
    return(max((Comparable)value,
            max(left.treeComp(), right.treeComp())));
}
```

23. Which of the following best describes what method treeComp does?

    A. Returns the largest value in its tree parameter
    B. Returns the largest value in a leaf of its tree parameter
    C. Returns the value in the root of its tree parameter
    D. Returns the value in the leftmost leaf in its tree parameter
    E. Returns the value in the rightmost leaf in its tree parameter

24. Assume that variable T is the root of a tree, every node of which contains the same kind of value. Consider the call T.treeComp(). The call will *not* cause a runtime error if the values in T have which of the following types?

    I. Object
    II. Integer
    III. String

    A. I only
    B. II only
    C. III only
    D. II and III only
    E. I, II, and III

25. Which of the following is a binary search tree?

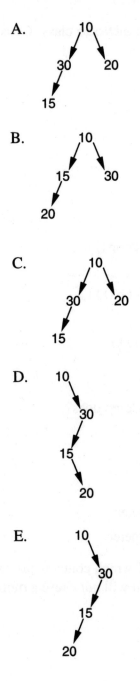

A. 10
30   20
15

B. 10
15   30
20

C. 10
30   20
15

D. 10
30
15
20

E. 10
30
15
20

26. Assume that doubly linked lists are implemented using the following (incomplete) class:

```
public class DblListNode {
    /*** fields ***/
    private Object value;
    private DblListNode previous;
    private DblListNode next;

    /*** methods ***/
    public void removeFromList() { method body }
}
```

Also assume that variables L and tmp are DblListNodes, with values as illustrated below.

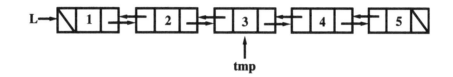

Which of the following code segments could be used to replace *method body* so that the call tmp.removeFromList() removes the node pointed to by tmp from the list pointed to by L?

A. `next = previous = null;`

B. `next = previous;`

C. `next = previous;`
   `previous = next;`

D. `next.previous = previous;`
   `previous.next = next;`
   `next = previous = null;`

E. `next.previous = previous.next;`
   `previous.next = next.previous;`
   `next = previous = null;`

27. Consider three different kinds of linked lists:

    1. A singly linked list with a pointer to the first node
    2. A doubly linked list with pointers to the first and last nodes
    3. A circular, doubly linked list with a pointer to the first node

    Assume that each list has N nodes. Which of the following best characterizes the times required, for each kind of list, to access the second-to-last node in the list?

	Singly linked, pointer to first node	Doubly linked, pointers to first and last nodes	Circular, doubly linked, pointer to first node
A.	$O(1)$	$O(1)$	$O(1)$
B.	$O(1)$	$O(N)$	$O(N)$
C.	$O(N)$	$O(1)$	$O(1)$
D.	$O(N)$	$O(N)$	$O(1)$
E.	$O(N)$	$O(N)$	$O(N)$

28. Consider the following code segment:

    ```
    String S = "happy";
    ListNode L = null;
    ListNode tmp = null;

    for (int k=0; k<S.length(); k++) {
        tmp = new ListNode(S.substring(k, k+1), L);
        L = tmp;
    }
    while (L != null) {
        System.out.print(L.getValue());
        L = L.getNext();
    }
    System.out.println();
    ```

    What will be printed when this code segment executes?

    A. happy

    B. happ

    C. yppah

    D. yppa

    E. Nothing will be printed.

Questions 29 and 30 rely on the following information:

Assume that binary trees are implemented using the standard `TreeNode` class. Two binary trees are considered to be equal if they are both empty or if the following three conditions all hold:

1. The values at the roots of the two trees are the same.
2. The left subtrees of the roots of the two trees are equal.
3. The right subtrees of the roots of the two trees are equal.

The method shown below was intended to determine whether its two binary tree parameters are equal. However, the method does not always work correctly. (Line numbers are included for reference.)

```
1. public static boolean treeEq(TreeNode T1, TreeNode T2) {
2.     if (T1 == null && T2 != null) || (T1 !=null && T2 == null)) {
3.         return false;
4.     }
5.     if (!T1.getValue().equals(T2.getValue())) {
6.         return false;
7.     }
8.     return(treeEq(T1.getLeft(), T2.getLeft()) &&
9.             treeEq(T1.getRight(), T2.getRight());
10. }
```

29. For which of the following values of `T1` and `T2` will method `treeEq` *fail* to work correctly?

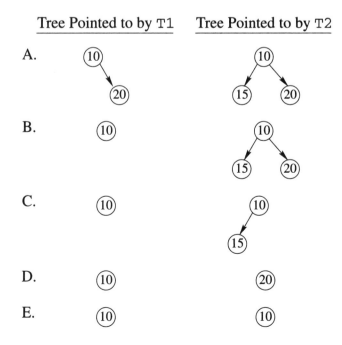

30. Which of the following changes fixes method `treeEq` so that it always works correctly?

    A. Before line 2, add `if (T1==null && T2==null) return true;`.

    B. Before line 2, add `if (T1==null || T2==null) return true;`.

    C. In line 2, change the `||` operator to the `&&` operator.

    D. Change line 3 to `return true;`.

    E. In line 8, change the `&&` operator to the `||` operator.

Questions 31 and 32 concern the following information:

Consider adding the following method to the `ListNode` class (line numbers are included for reference).

```
1. public boolean listLookup(Object ob) {
2.     ListNode tmp = next;
3.     if (value.equals(ob)) return true;
4.     while (!tmp.value.equals(ob) && tmp != null) {
5.         tmp = tmp.next;
6.     }
7.     return (tmp.value.equals(ob));
8. }
```

Given a `ListNode L` that is the first node in a linked list, the call `L.listLookup(ob)` was intended to return true if and only if `ob` is in the linked list. However, calling the method sometimes causes a runtime error due to an attempt to dereference a null pointer.

31. Under which of the following circumstances does a call to `listLookup` cause a runtime error?

    I. Value `ob` is not in the list.
    II. Value `ob` is the last value in the list.
    III. Value `ob` is the second-to-last value in the list.

    A. I only

    B. II only

    C. III only

    D. I and II only

    E. II and III only

32. Which of the following changes could be used to fix method `listLookup` so that it always works as intended?

    A. Change line 4 to `while (tmp != null &&`
       `!tmp.getValue().equals(ob))`.

    B. Change line 4 to `while (tmp != null &&`
       `!tmp.getValue().equals(ob))`
       and change line 7 to `return (tmp != null);`.

    C. Change line 4 to `while (tmp != null &&`
       `!tmp.getValue().equals(ob))`
       and change line 7 to `return (tmp == null);`.

    D. Change line 7 to `return (tmp != null);`.

    E. Change line 7 to `return (tmp != null &&`
       `tmp.getValue().equals(ob));`.

33. Consider adding a new version of the `add` method to the `ap.java.util.LinkedList` class. The header for the new method is shown below.

    ```
    public void add(Object x, boolean toFront)
    ```

    If parameter `toFront` is `true`, the new method would add x to the front of the list; otherwise, it would add x to the end of the list.

    Which of the following statements about this proposal is true?

    A. The new method cannot be added to the `LinkedList` class because that class already has a method with the same name.

    B. The new method cannot be added to the `LinkedList` class because that class already has an `add` method with a parameter of type `Object`.

    C. The new method as defined above cannot be added to the `LinkedList` class; however, if both parameters were `Object`s, the new method could be added to the `LinkedList` class.

    D. The new method as defined above cannot be added to the `LinkedList` class; however, if the parameters were specified in the opposite order, `public void add(boolean toFront, Object x)`, the new method could be added to the `LinkedList` class.

    E. The new method can be added to the `LinkedList` class because the existing `add` method only has one parameter whereas the new method has two.

Questions 34–36 concern the following algorithm, which copies values from an array into a binary search tree and then prints the values, using an inorder traversal of the tree.

Step 1:

Initialize the tree to be empty.

Step 2:

For each value in the array from left to right, insert the value into the tree.

Step 3:

Print the values in the tree using an inorder traversal.

34. Which of the following best describes the sequence of values printed by step 3 of the algorithm?

    A. The values are printed in sorted order.

    B. The values are printed in random order.

    C. The values are printed in the same order in which they occur in the array.

    D. The values are printed in the reverse of the order in which they occur in the array.

    E. The smallest value is printed first, then the largest value, then the second smallest, then the second largest, and so on.

35. Assume that the array contains N values. Which of the following best characterizes the worst-case running time of the algorithm?

    A. $O(1)$

    B. $O(\log N)$

    C. $O(N)$

    D. $O(N \log N)$

    E. $O(N^2)$

36. The algorithm is guaranteed to exhibit its worst-case running time under which of the following conditions?

    A. The array contains only positive values.

    B. The array contains only negative values.

    C. Half of the values in the array are positive and half are negative.

    D. The values are stored in the array in sorted order.

    E. The values are stored in the array in nonsorted order.

37. Assume that priority queues of Integers are implemented using the following (incomplete) class definition:

    ```
    public class IntPriorityQueue implements PriorityQueue {
        implementation omitted
    }
    ```

    Also assume that A is an array of Integers. Consider the following code segment:

    ```
    PriorityQueue PQ = new IntPriorityQueue();
    for (int k=0; k<A.length; k++) {
        PQ.add(A[k]);
    }
    while (!PQ.isEmpty()) {
        Integer oneInt = (Integer)PQ.removeMin();
        System.out.println(oneInt.intValue());
    }
    ```

    Assume that array A contains *N* values. What is printed when this code segment executes?

    A.   The values 0 to *N* − 1

    B.   A's *N* values in the order in which they occur in A

    C.   A's *N* values in the *reverse* of the order in which they occur in A

    D.   A's *N* values in sorted order from smallest to largest

    E.   A's *N* values in sorted order from largest to smallest

38.   Which of the following is *not* a min-heap?

A.

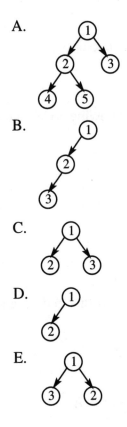

B.

C.

D.

E.

39.   Consider adding the following recursive method to the standard `ListNode` class:

```
public boolean checkList() {
    int val1, val2;

    if (next == null) return true;
    if (value.compareTo(next.value) > 0) return false;
    return(next.checkList());
}
```

Which of the following best characterizes the lists for which method `checkList` returns `true`?

A.   Lists that contain duplicate values

B.   Lists that contain at least one positive value

C.   Lists that contain at least one negative value

D.   Lists that are sorted in ascending order

E.   Lists that are sorted in descending order

40. Assume that L is a ListNode that represents a linked list of Integers as shown below.

    $$L \to 0 \to 5 \to 2 \to 9 \to 1$$

    Consider the following code segment:

    ```
    ListNode tmp;
    ListNode newList = null;

    while (L != null) {
        tmp = L.getNext();
        if (((Integer)L.getValue()).intValue() < 3) {
            L.setNext(newList);
            newList = L;
        }
        L = tmp;
    }
    ```

    Which of the following correctly shows the value of newList after the code segment executes?

    A. newList $\to 2$
    B. newList $\to 0 \to 2 \to 1$
    C. newList $\to 1 \to 2 \to 0$
    D. newList $\to 0 \to 1 \to 2$
    E. newList $\to 2 \to 1 \to 0$

AB Practice Examination 1

Section II

Time — 1 hour and 45 minutes
Number of questions — 4
Percent of total grade — 50

Question 1

The Orchard class partially defined below is used to represent a kiwi orchard in which the kiwi vines are planted in a rectangular grid. Grid coordinates are represented using the Point class, also defined below.

```
import ap.java.util.ArrayList;

public class Point {
    /*** fields ***/
    private int x;
    private int y;

    /*** methods ***/
    // constructor
    public Point(int initX, int initY) {
        x = initX;
        y = initY;
    }

    public int getX() { return x; }
    public int getY() { return y; }
}

public class Orchard {
    /*** fields ***/
    private String[][] plants; // each array element is either
                               // "male" or "female"

    /*** methods ***/
    public boolean willFruit( Point p ) { ... }
    public ArrayList willNotFruit() { ... }
}
```

Each kiwi plant is either male or female. The `plants` array (which is a private field of the `Orchard` class) keeps track of the genders of the plants in the orchard: each element of the array contains a string, either `"male"` or `"female"`, depending on the gender of the plant in that position.

In order to produce fruit, a female plant must have a male plant no more than two positions away horizontally or vertically, or no more than one position away diagonally. For example, consider the orchard represented using the following array:

male	female	female	female	female
female	female	female	female	male
female	**female**	**female**	female	female

In this orchard, the plants shown in bold (in positions (2,1) and (2,2)) will not produce fruit because no male plant is close enough to them.

Part (a)

Write the body of the `Orchard` class's `willFruit` method as started below. The method returns `true` if and only if the female plant at the given position will produce fruit.

```
public boolean willFruit( Point p ) {
// precondition: Point p is inside the plants array and
//               the plant at position p is female
```

Part (b)

Write the body of the `Orchard` class's `willNotFruit` method as started below. The method returns an `ArrayList` containing the positions (`Points`) of all of the female plants in the orchard that will not fruit. For example, for the orchard shown above, the method would return a list containing two `Points` representing the positions (2,1) and (2,2).

In writing method `willNotFruit`, you may include calls to method `willFruit`, defined above in Part (a). Assume that method `willFruit` works as specified, regardless of what you wrote for Part (a).

Complete method `willNotFruit` below.

```
public ArrayList willNotFruit() {
\\ postcondition: returns an ArrayList containing the positions
\\                (Points) of all of the female plants in the
\\                orchard that will not fruit
```

Question 2

This question involves the two classes partially defined below. The `Person` class is used to store information about one person; the `Family` class is used to store information about a family (containing zero or more people). The `Family` class contains a `ListNode` field that is either null or points to the first node of a linked list of the people in the family, sorted by age (from youngest to oldest).

```
public class Person {
    /*** fields ***/
    private String name;
    private int age;

    /*** methods ***/
    // constructor
    public Person(String theName, int theAge) {
        name = theName;
        age = theAge;
    }
    public String getName() { return name; }
    public int getAge() { return age; }
}

public class Family {
    /*** fields ***/
    private ListNode peopleList;     // pointer to linked list of
                                     // people in this family,
                                     // sorted by age (from youngest
                                     // to oldest)

    /*** public methods ***/
    public Family() {                // constructor
        peopleList = null;
    }
    public void addPerson(Person p) { ... }  // adds person p to
                                             // this family

    /*** private methods ***/
    private ListNode personBefore(int age) { ... }
}
```

Part (a)

Write the `personBefore` method of the `Family` class, as started below. Method `personBefore` should search through the linked list pointed to by `peopleList`, looking for the person whose age is closest to the value of parameter `age` without being larger. It should return a pointer to that node of the linked list. If there is no such person (i.e., if the linked list is empty or all ages are greater than the value of parameter `age`), method `personBefore` should return `null`.

Complete method `personBefore` below.

```
private ListNode personBefore(int age) {
// precondition: the peopleList field is null, or it points to the
//               first node of a linked list;
//               the list is sorted according to the ages of the
//               people in the list (from youngest to oldest)
//
// postcondition:  returns a pointer to the node in the linked list
//                 for the person in this family whose age is closest
//                 to the given age without being larger;
//                 returns null if there are no people in this family
//                 at all, or none whose age is less than or equal to
//                 the given age
```

Part (b)

Write the `addPerson` method of the `Family` class, as started below. Method `addPerson` should add person p to the family, so that the family's list of people is still sorted by age (from youngest to oldest).

In writing method `addPerson`, you may include calls to method `personBefore`, specified above in Part (a). Assume that `personBefore` works as specified, regardless of what you wrote in Part (a).

Complete method `addPerson` below.

```
public void addPerson(Person p) {
// precondition: the peopleList field is null, or it points to the
//               first node of a linked list;
//               the list is sorted according to the ages of the
//               people in the list (from youngest to oldest)
// postcondition: p has been added to the linked list in sorted
//                order (by age)
```

Question 3

This question involves binary trees and doubly linked lists, both implemented using the following Node class:

```
public class Node {
    /*** fields ***/
    private Object data;
    private Node left;      // for a tree, root of left subtree;
                            // for a doubly linked list, previous node
    private Node right;     // for a tree, root of right subtree;
                            // for a doubly linked list, next node

    /*** methods ***/
    // constructor
    public Node(Object dataVal, Node leftVal, Node rightVal) {
        data = dataVal;
        left = leftVal;
        right = rightVal;
    }
    public Object getData() { return data; }
    public Node getLeft() { return left; }
    public Node getRight() { return right; }
    public void setLeft(Node newLeft) { left = newLeft; }
    public void setRight(Node newRight) { right = newRight; }

    public Node lastNode( ) {
    // precondition: this Node is the first node in a doubly
    //               linked list
    // postcondition: returns the last node in the list
        ...
    }

    public Node treeToList( ) {
    // precondition: this Node is the root of a binary tree
    // postcondition: converts the tree to a doubly linked list,
    //                and returns the first node in the list
        ...
    }
}
```

Part (a)

Write the `lastNode` method of the `Node` class. Method `lastNode` should return the last node in the doubly linked list.

Complete method `lastNode` below.

```
public Node lastNode( ) {
// precondition: this Node is the first node in a doubly linked list
// postcondition: returns the last node in the list
```

Part (b)

Write the `treeToList` method of the `Node` class. Method `treeToList` should convert the binary tree rooted at the `Node` whose method was called to a doubly linked list as explained below, and it should return the first node in the list.

The following algorithm should be used to convert a binary tree rooted at node `T` to a doubly linked list:

1. Recursively convert `T`'s left and right subtrees to doubly linked lists `L1` and `L2`, respectively (a `null` subtree should be converted to a `null` list).

2. If `L1` is not `null`, set the `right` field of the last node in list `L1` to be node `T`, and set the `left` field of node `T` to be the last node in list `L1`.

3. If `L2` is not `null`, set the `left` field of the first node in list `L2` to be node `T`, and set the `right` field of node `T` to be the first node in list `L2`.

4. If `L1` is not `null`, return the first node in list `L1`; otherwise, return node `T`.

For example:

Tree with Root Node T   Result of the Call `T.treeToList()`

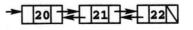

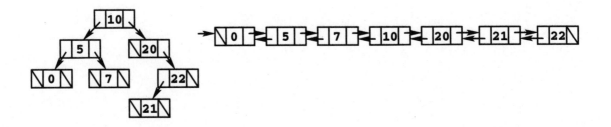

To receive full credit for this question, the linked list created by your code must occupy the same storage as the binary tree. You must only modify the `left` and `right` fields of the nodes; you must not allocate new storage for the list nodes.

In writing method `treeToList`, you may include calls to method `lastNode`, specified above in Part (a). Assume that `lastNode` works as specified, regardless of what you wrote for Part (a).

Complete method `treeToList` below.

```
public Node treeToList( ) {
// precondition: T is the root of a binary tree
// postcondition: converts the tree to a doubly linked list, and
//                returns the first node in the list
```

Question 4

This question assumes that binary trees are implemented using the following (partially specified) `TreeNode` class:

```java
public class TreeNode {
    /*** fields ***/
    private int level;
    private TreeNode left;
    private TreeNode right;

    /*** methods ***/
    public void setLevels() { ... }
    public int highestLevelNum() { ... }
}
```

Part (a)

Write the `setLevels` method of the `TreeNode` class. Method `setLevels` should fill in the `level` fields of all of the nodes in the tree rooted at the node whose `setLevels` method is called as follows:

- The root node should have `level` 1.

- For all nodes *n*: if *n* has `level` *k*, then *n*'s children (if any) should have `level` $k+1$

For example:

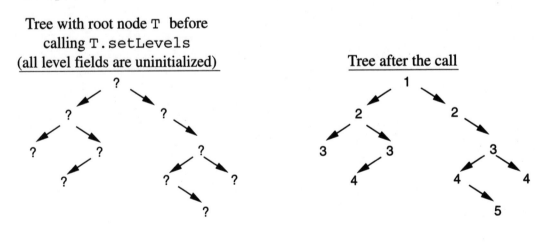

Complete method `setLevels` below. You may find it helpful to write an auxiliary method (a private method of the `TreeNode` class) with one integer parameter: the level number to be assigned to the root node.

```
public void setLevels( ) {
```

Part (b)

Write the `highestLevelNum` method of the `TreeNode` class. Method `highestLevelNum` should return the highest level number in the tree. (Assume that the `level` fields of all of the nodes in the tree have been filled in correctly.)

For example, if `T` is as shown above in Part (a) after the call `T.setLevels()`, then the call `T.highestLevelNum()` should return 5.

Complete method `highestLevelNum` below.

```
public int highestLevelNum( ) {
// precondition: the level fields of all nodes have been filled
//                in correctly
```

Answers to AB Practice Examination 1

Section I

1.	A	21.	B
2.	E	22.	D
3.	E	23.	A
4.	D	24.	D
5.	C	25.	D
6.	C	26.	D
7.	B	27.	C
8.	E	28.	C
9.	C	29.	E
10.	D	30.	A
11.	C	31.	A
12.	A	32.	B
13.	B	33.	E
14.	D	34.	A
15.	B	35.	E
16.	E	36.	D
17.	D	37.	D
18.	A	38.	B
19.	A	39.	D
20.	C	40.	C

Answers to AB Practice Examination 1

Section II

Question 1

Part (a)

Note that method `willFruit` is much easier to write if you first write an auxiliary method that tests one position of the array to see whether that position is inside the `plants` array and, if so, contains a male plant:

```
private boolean isMale(int x, int y) {
    if (x < 0 || x >= plants.length ||
        y < 0 || y >= plants[0].length) return false;
    return( plants[x][y].equals("male"));
}
```

This auxiliary method is used by both versions of the `willFruit` method given below.

Version 1

Check each position explicitly.

```
public boolean willFruit( Point p ) {
    return(isMale(p.getX(), p.getY()-1) ||
           isMale(p.getX(), p.getY()+1) ||
           isMale(p.getX()-1, p.getY()) ||
           isMale(p.getX()-1, p.getY()-1) ||
           isMale(p.getX()-1, p.getY()+1) ||
           isMale(p.getX()+1, p.getY()) ||
           isMale(p.getX()+1, p.getY()-1) ||
           isMale(p.getX()+1, p.getY()+1) ||
           isMale(p.getX()+2, p.getY()) ||
           isMale(p.getX()-2, p.getY()) ||
           isMale(p.getX(), p.getY()+2) ||
           isMale(p.getX(), p.getY()-2));
}
```

Version 2

Use a loop to check all positions one step away (horizontally, vertically, or diagonally), then check all positions two steps away horizontally or vertically.

```java
public boolean willFruit( Point p ) {
    int x = p.getX();
    int y = p.getY();

    // check one step away
    for (int row=x-1; row<=x+1; row++) {
        for (int col=y-1; col<=y+1; col++) {
            if (isMale(row, col)) return true;
        }
    }

    // check two steps away horizontally or vertically
    return(isMale(p.getX()+2, p.getY()) ||
           isMale(p.getX()-2, p.getY()) ||
           isMale(p.getX(), p.getY()+2) ||
           isMale(p.getX(), p.getY()-2));
}
```

Common errors:

- Code that can cause an out-of-bounds array index
- Checking positions two steps away diagonally

Part (b)

```java
public ArrayList willNotFruit() {
    ArrayList L = new ArrayList();

    for (int j=0; j<plants.length; j++) {
        for (int k=0; k<plants[0].length; k++) {
            if (plants[j][k].equals("female")) {
                Point p = new Point(j,k);
                if (!willFruit(p)) {
                    L.add(p);
                }
            }
        }
    }
    return L;
}
```

Question 2

Part (a)

```
private ListNode personBefore(int age) {
// precondition: the peopleList field is null, or it points to the
//                first node of a linked list;
//                the list is sorted according to the ages of the
//                people in the list (from youngest to oldest)
//
// postcondition:  returns a pointer to the node in the linked list
//                 for the person in this family whose age is closest
//                 to the given age without being larger;
//                 returns null if there are no people in this family
//                 at all, or none whose age is less than or equal to
//                 the given age
    ListNode tmp = peopleList;
    Person currentPerson;

    // return null if no one in the list has age <= given age
    if (tmp == null) return null;
    currentPerson = (Person)tmp.getValue();
    if (currentPerson.getAge() > age) return null;

    // there is at least one person whose age is less than or equal
    // to the given age; find the oldest such person
    while (tmp.getNext() != null) {
        // return current ListNode if next person's age > given age,
        // else go on to next node in list
        currentPerson = ((Person)tmp.getNext().getValue());
        if (currentPerson.getAge() > age) return tmp;
        tmp = tmp.getNext();
    }
    // here if all people in the list have ages <= given age;
    // return the last node in the list
    return tmp;
}
```

Common errors:

- Incorrect checks for no one in the list whose age is less than or equal to the given age
- Incorrect loop termination condition (causing a `NullPointerException`)
- Accessing private fields (e.g., the myAge field of the `Person` class or the `value` field of the `ListNode` class) directly rather than using the appropriate method

Part (b)

```
public void addPerson(Person p) {
// precondition: the peopleList field is null, or it points to the
//                first node of a linked list;
//                the list is sorted according to the ages of the
//                people in the list (from youngest to oldest)
// postcondition: p has been added to the linked list in sorted
//                   order (by age)
    ListNode n = personBefore(p.getAge());
    if (n == null) {
        // add p at front of list
        ListNode newNode = new ListNode(p, peopleList);
        peopleList = newNode;
    }
    else {
        // add p after node n
        ListNode newNode = new ListNode(p, n.getNext());
        n.setNext(newNode);
    }
}
```

Common errors:

- Bad call to `personBefore` (e.g., passing p instead of `p.getAge()`)
- Forgetting to check whether the value returned by `personBefore` is `null`
- Setting the `next` field of the new node to `null` in all cases
- Forgetting to set `peopleList` and/or the `next` field of node n to point to the new node

Question 3

Part (a)

```
public Node lastNode( ) {
// precondition: this Node is the first node in a doubly linked list
// postcondition: returns the last node in the list
    if (right == null) return this;
    return right.lastNode();
}
```

Part (b)

```
public Node treeToList( ) {
// precondition: this Node is the root of a binary tree
// postcondition: converts the tree to a doubly linked list,
//                 and returns the first node in the list
    Node L1, L2;

    // convert left and right subtrees to lists
    if (left==null) L1 = null;
    else L1 = left.treeToList();
    if (right==null) L2 = null;
    else L2 = right.treeToList();

    // set the fields
    if (L1 != null) {
        Node last = L1.lastNode();
        last.setRight(this);
        left = last;
    }
    if (L2 != null) {
        L2.setLeft(this);
        right = L2;
    }

    // return the list
    if (L1 != null) return L1;
    else return this;
}
```

Question 4

Part (a)

```
private void setLevelsAux(int k) {
    level = k;
    if (left != null) left.setLevelsAux(k+1);
    if (right != null) right.setLevelsAux(k+1);
}

public void setLevels() {
    setLevelsAux(1);
}
```

Part (b)

For this part of the question, it is convenient to define an auxiliary function named max that returns the larger of its two integer parameters.

```
private static int max(int j, int k) {
    if (j > k) return j;
    return k;
}

public int highestLevelNum() {
    if (left == null && right == null) return level;
    else if (left == null) return right.highestLevel();
    else if (right == null) return left.highestLevel();
    else return max(left.highestLevel(), right.highestLevel());
}
```

AB Practice Examination 2

Section I

Time — 1 hour and 15 minutes
Number of questions — 40
Percent of total grade — 50

1. Assume that A is a nonempty array of `ints`. Consider the following code segment:

```
int x = 0;
for (int k=1; k<A.length; k++) {
    if (A[k] < A[x]) x = k;
}
return A[x];
```

Which of the following best describes what this code segment does?

A. It returns the index of the smallest element of A.

B. It returns the index of the largest element of A.

C. It returns the value of the smallest element of A.

D. It returns the value of the largest element of A.

E. It is not possible to determine what the code segment does without knowing how A is initialized.

2. Which of the following is a valid reason for using a singly linked list rather than a doubly linked list?

   A. Less storage is required for a singly linked list than for a doubly linked list.

   B. A singly linked list can be used to implement a queue, whereas a doubly linked list cannot.

   C. The number of items in the list can be determined more efficiently using a singly linked list than using a doubly linked list.

   D. The average of the values in the list can be computed more efficiently using a singly linked list than using a doubly linked list.

   E. Given a pointer to one of the nodes in the list, it is possible to determine whether it is the last node if the list is singly linked, but not if it is doubly linked.

3. Assume that the following recursive method has been added to the standard `ListNode` class:

   ```
   public int listCompute( ) {
       if (next == null) return 1;
       return(1 + next.listCompute( ));
   }
   ```

   Which of the following best describes what method `listCompute` does?

   A. Returns the sum of the values in the list

   B. Returns the average of the values in the list

   C. Returns the largest value in the list

   D. Returns the smallest value in the list

   E. Returns the number of nodes in the list

4. Which node of a binary tree is the first node visited by a preorder traversal?

   A. The root node

   B. The leftmost leaf

   C. The rightmost leaf

   D. The node that contains the largest value

   E. The node that contains the smallest value

5. Consider the following recursive method (assume that method `readInt` reads the next integer value from a file):

```
public static void printVals(int n) {
    if (n > 0) {
        int x = readInt();
        printVals(n-1);
        if (x > 0) System.out.print(x + " ");
    }
}
```

Assume that the input file contains the values:

```
10  -10  20  -20  30  -30
```

What is printed as a result of the call `printVals(3)`?

A. 10 20

B. 20 10

C. 10 20 30

D. 10 -10 20

E. 20 -10 10

6. Assume that the following method has been added to the standard `TreeNode` class:

```
public int treeCount() {
    if ((left == null) && (right == null)) return 0;
    if (left == null) return(1 + right.treeCount());
    if (right == null) return(1 + left.treeCount());
    return(1 + left.treeCount() + right.treeCount());
}
```

Which of the following best describes what method `treeCount` does?

A. Always returns 0

B. Returns the number of nodes in the tree

C. Returns the number of leaves in the tree

D. Returns the number of nonleaves in the tree

E. Returns the height of the tree

7. Assume that variable S is a stack of `Integers` and that Q is a queue of `Integers`, initialized as shown below.

	Top			**Bottom**			**Front**			**Rear**
S:	2	4	6	8		Q:	1	3	5	7

Consider the following code segment:

```
Object ob;
while (!S.empty()) {
    ob = S.pop();
    Q.enqueue(ob);
}
while (!Q.empty()) {
    ob = Q.dequeue();
    S.push(ob);
}
```

Which of the following best illustrates the values of S and Q after the code segment executes?

	S		Q	
	Top ... **Bottom**		**Front** ... **Rear**	

A.
S: 2 4 6 8
Q: 1 3 5 7

B.
S: 1 3 5 7
Q: 2 4 6 8

C.
S: 2 4 6 8 1 3 5 7
Q: (empty)

D.
S: 1 3 5 7 2 4 6 8
Q: (empty)

E.
S: 8 6 4 2 7 5 3 1
Q: (empty)

8. Assume that variable S is a stack of `Integers` and that Q is a queue of `Integers`, initialized as shown below.

	Top		**Bottom**			**Front**		**Rear**
S:	2	4	6	8	Q:	1	3	5	7

Consider the following code segment:

```
Object ob;
while (!Q.empty()) {
    ob = Q.dequeue();
    S.push(ob);
}
while (!S.empty()) {
    ob = S.pop();
    Q.enqueue(ob);
}
```

Which of the following best illustrates the values of S and Q after the code segment executes?

	S			Q						
	Top **Bottom**			**Front**						**Rear**
A.	2 4 6 8			1	3	5	7			
B.	1 3 5 7			2	4	6	8			
C.	(empty)			7	5	3	1	2	4	6 8
D.	(empty)			1	3	5	7	2	4	6 8
E.	(empty)			8	6	4	2	1	3	5 7

Questions 9 and 10 refer to the following information:

Assume that the following method has been added to the `ListNode` class:

```
public boolean checkList(Comparable v) {
// precondition: The values in this list are comparable to v
//                and are in sorted order (low to high).
    if (v.compareTo((Comparable)value) == 0) return true;
    if (v.compareTo((Comparable)value) < 0) return false;
    return next.checkList(v);
}
```

9. When does method `checkList` cause a runtime error due to an attempt to dereference a null pointer?

   A. Never
   B. Whenever the value v is somewhere in the list
   C. Whenever the value v is *not* in the list
   D. Whenever a value greater than v is somewhere in the list
   E. Whenever a value less than v is somewhere in the list

10. When does method `checkList` return `true`?

    A. When the value v is somewhere in the list
    B. Only when the value v is the first value in the list
    C. Only when the value v is the last value in the list
    D. When a value greater than v is somewhere in the list
    E. Only when a value greater than v is the first value in the list

11. Assume that the following method has been added to the `TreeNode` class:

```
public void mystery( Stack S ) {
    if (right != null) right.mystery(S);
    S.push(value);
    if (left != null) left.mystery(S);
}
```

Assume that T is a `TreeNode` that is the root of a binary search tree, and that T's `mystery` method is initially called with an empty stack S. Which of the following best describes S after the call?

A. S is empty.

B. S contains only the value at the root of the tree.

C. S contains all of the values in the tree in unsorted order.

D. S contains all of the values in the tree in sorted order; the smallest value is at the top of the stack.

E. S contains all of the values in the tree in sorted order; the largest value is at the top of the stack.

12. Consider the following code segment:

```
x = !y;
y = !x;
x = !y;
```

Assume that x and y are initialized boolean variables. Which of the following statements is true?

A. The final value of x is the same as the initial value of x.

B. The final value of x is the same as the initial value of y.

C. The final value of y is the same as the initial value of y.

D. The final value of y is the same as the initial value of x.

E. It is not possible to say anything about the final values of x and y without knowing their initial values.

13. Assume that two classes, Plant and Animal, and two interfaces, Tropical and Spotted, have been defined. Consider defining a new class named Mold. Which of the following statements is true?

   A. The Mold class can extend at most one of the Plant and Animal classes, and it can implement at most one of the Tropical and Spotted interfaces.

   B. The Mold class can extend at most one of the Plant and Animal classes, but it can implement both the Tropical and Spotted interfaces.

   C. The Mold class can extend both the Plant and Animal classes, but it can implement at most one of the Tropical and Spotted interfaces.

   D. The Mold class can extend both the Plant and Animal classes, and it can implement both the Tropical and Spotted interfaces.

   E. If the Mold class implements both the Tropical and Spotted interfaces, it can extend at most one of the Plant and Animal classes. If it implements just one of the Tropical and Spotted interfaces, it can extend both the Plant and Animal classes.

14. Consider the following class definition:

```
public class Node {
    /*** fields ***/
    private Object data;
    private Node left;
    private Node right;

    /*** methods ***/
    public void change() {
        left = right;
        right = left;
    }
}
```

Assume that variable X is a Node, initialized as shown below.

Which of the following best illustrates the result of the call X.change()?

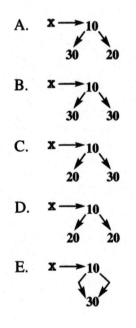

A. X → 10
     30   20

B. X → 10
     30   30

C. X → 10
     20   30

D. X → 10
     20   20

E. X → 10
       30

Questions 15 and 16 concern the following two possibilities for a data structure to be used to store students' grades on an exam. There are N students, and each grade is an integer in the range 0 to 100.

Data Structure 1:

Use an array A of length 101 (each element of the array corresponds to one possible grade). For each value of k from 0 to 100, A[k] contains a linked list of strings: the names of the students who got grade k on the exam.

Data Structure 2:

Use an array A of length N (each element of the array corresponds to one student). For each value of k from 0 to N-1, A[k] contains a Student object that has two fields: the name of the kth student and that student's grade. The Students are stored in the array in sorted order according to the students' names.

The data structure will be used to support three operations:

I. Given a student's name, look up that student's exam grade.
II. Given the names of two students, determine whether they got the same grade.
III. Print the names of all the students who got 100 on the exam.

15. Which of the three operations could be performed more efficiently using Data Structure 1 than using Data Structure 2?

A. I only
B. II only
C. III only
D. I and II
E. II and III

16. Which of the three operations could be performed more efficiently using Data Structure 2 than using Data Structure 1?

A. I only
B. II only
C. III only
D. I and II
E. II and III

17. Consider writing a method to move N values from the front of an array to the end of the array. For example, the figure below illustrates moving three values in an array; the values that are moved are shown in bold italic font for emphasis.

Original array	After moving three values
10 14 12 17 13 19 20	17 13 19 20 ***10 14 12***

Assume that the method works as follows:

Repeat N times:

- Save the value at the front of the array in a temporary variable.
- Move all values in the array one place to the left.
- Put the saved value into the last position in the array.

If the array contains M values, which of the following best characterizes the running time of the method?

A. $O(M)$

B. $O(N)$

C. $O(M+N)$

D. $O(M*N)$

E. $O(M^N)$

Questions 18–20 rely on the following information:

Assume that the two methods partially specified below have been added to the `TreeNode` class.

```
public boolean lookup(Object ob) {
// postcondition: Returns true if value ob is in the tree rooted at
//                this node; otherwise, returns false.
    ...
}

public boolean subset(TreeNode T) {
// precondition: T is not null
// postcondition: returns true if every value in the tree rooted
//                at this node is also in the tree rooted at T;
//                otherwise, returns false
    if (! T.lookup(value)) return false;
    if (left == null && right == null) return true;
    if (left == null) return right.subset(T);
    else if (right == null) return left.subset(T);
    else MISSING CODE
}
```

18. Assume that method `lookup` has been implemented correctly. Which of the following could be used to replace *MISSING CODE* in method `subset` so that it works as specified by its pre- and postcondition?

    A. `return true;`

    B. `return (left.subset(T) && right.subset(T));`

    C. `return (left.subset(T) || right.subset(T));`

    D. `return (left.subset(T.getLeft()) &&`
       `        right.subset(T.getRight()));`

    E. `return (left.subset(T.getLeft()) ||`
       `        right.subset(T.getRight()));`

19. Assume that the `subset` method has been implemented correctly. Consider adding an `equals` method to the `TreeNode` class to be used to determine when two binary trees are the same. Two trees are considered to be the same when they contain exactly the same values (even if the values are stored in different places in the two trees). Which of the following versions of the `equals` method work(s) correctly?

    Version I:
    ```
    public boolean equals(TreeNode T) {
        if (!subset(T)) return false;
        return (T.subset(this));
    }
    ```

    Version II:
    ```
    public boolean equals(TreeNode T) {
        return (subset(T) && T.subset(this) );
    }
    ```

    Version III:
    ```
    public boolean equals(TreeNode T) {
        return (subset(T) || T.subset(this) );
    }
    ```

    A. I only

    B. II only

    C. III only

    D. I and II

    E. I and III

20. Assume that the `equals` method defined in the previous question has been implemented correctly and that T1 and T2 are both nonnull `TreeNodes`. Which of the following correctly characterizes the conditions under which the two expressions T1 == T2 and T1.equals(T2) both evaluate to `true`?

    A. Always

    B. Never

    C. Whenever the two variables both point to the same chunk of storage

    D. Whenever the trees rooted at T1 and T2 are both binary search trees containing the same values

    E. Whenever the trees rooted at T1 and T2 have the same shape and contain the same values

21. Assume that A is a nonempty rectangular array of `ints`. Consider the following code segment:

```
for (int col=0; col<A[0].length; col++) {
    for (int row=0; row<A.length-1; row++) {
        if (A[row][col] > A[row+1][col]) return false;
    }
}
return true;
```

Which of the following best describes when this code segment returns true?

A. When every row of A is sorted in increasing order

B. When no row of A contains duplicate values

C. When every column of A is sorted in increasing order

D. When no column of A contains duplicate values

E. When neither diagonal of A contains duplicate values

22. Which of the following is a valid reason for choosing to store a sequence of values in an array rather than in a linked list?

A. It is possible to store values of any type in an array, but only scalar values can be stored in a linked list.

B. An array can be returned as the result of a method call, but a linked list cannot.

C. The value in the kth position in the array can be accessed in O(1) time, whereas accessing the value in the kth node of a linked list requires O(k) time.

D. A new value can be added to the beginning of an array of size N in O(1) time, whereas adding a new value to the front of a linked list with N nodes requires O(N) time in the worst case.

E. The value at the beginning of an array of size N can be removed in O(1) time, whereas removing the first node from a linked list with N nodes requires O(N) time in the worst case.

Questions 23 and 24 refer to the following recursive method:

```
public static int compute(int x, int y) {
    if (x > y) return x;
    else return( compute(x+2, y-2) );
}
```

23. What is returned by the call `compute(1, 5)`?

    A. 1
    B. 3
    C. 5
    D. 7
    E. No value is returned because an infinite recursion occurs.

24. Which of the following best characterizes the circumstances under which the call `compute(x, y)` leads to an infinite recursion?

    A. Never
    B. Whenever x = y
    C. Whenever x < y
    D. Whenever x > y
    E. Whenever both x and y are odd

25. Consider the following two ways to store a set of N integer values.

    Method 1:

    Store the values in sorted order in an array of length N.

    Method 2:

    Store the values in a binary search tree.

    Which of the following describes a valid reason to prefer Method 1 over Method 2?

    A. Computing the sum of the values can be done in O($\log N$) time using Method 1, but it will require O(N) time in the worst case using Method 2.
    B. Determining whether a given value is in the set can be done in O(1) time using Method 1, but it will require O(N^2) time in the worst case using Method 2.
    C. Printing the smallest value in the set can be done in O(1) time using Method 1, but it will require O(N) time in the worst case using Method 2.
    D. Printing all values in sorted order can be done in O(N) time using Method 1, but it will require O($N \log N$) time in the worst case using Method 2.
    E. Method 1 requires O(N) space, whereas Method 2 requires O($N \log N$) space in the worst case.

26. Assume that linked lists of `Integers` are implemented using the standard `ListNode` class, and that the following method has been added to the `ListNode` class. (Line numbers are included for reference.)

    ```
    1. public int ListNode search(){
    2. int k = ((Integer)value).intValue();
    3.     if (k <= 0) return k;
    4.     if (next == null) return 1;
    5.     return next.search();
    6. }
    ```

    Which of the following best describes what method `search` does?

    A. Always returns 1
    B. Returns the first positive value in the list, or 1 if there is no such value
    C. Returns the last positive value in the list, or 1 if there is no such value
    D. Returns the first nonpositive value in the list, or 1 if there is no such value
    E. Returns the last nonpositive value in the list, or 1 if there is no such value

27. Which of the following operations can be implemented more efficiently (in terms of worst-case time) on a sorted array of integers than on an unsorted array of integers?

    A. Searching for a given value in the array

    B. Adding a new value to the array

    C. Removing a value from the array

    D. Printing all values in the array

    E. Computing the sum of all values in the array

Questions 28 and 29 concern the following information:

A company has locations in 1,000 cities. The company has 100 managers, each in charge of some set of cities. The following two data structures are being considered to store information about the cities handled by each manager:

Data Structure 1:

    A two-dimensional array A of booleans. The rows of A correspond to the managers, and the columns of A correspond to the cities. Entry A[j][k] is true if and only if manager j handles city k.

Data Structure 2:

    A one-dimensional array A of linked lists. The list in A[j] contains the numbers of the cities handled by manager j.

28. Which of the following operations can be implemented more efficiently using Data Structure 1 than using Data Structure 2?

    A. Determine whether a given manager handles a given city.

    B. Determine how many cities are handled by a given manager.

    C. Determine whether any manager handles no cities.

    D. Determine which manager handles the most cities.

    E. Print the list of cities handled by a given manager.

29. Which of the following operations can be implemented more efficiently using Data Structure 2 than using Data Structure 1?

    A. Determine which manager handles a given city.

    B. Determine whether a given manager handles more than one city.

    C. Remove a given city from the set handled by a given manager.

    D. Add a given city to the set handled by a given manager.

    E. Change the manager of a given city.

30. Assume that variable A is a nonempty `ArrayList`. Consider the following statement:

    ```
    String s = (String)A.get(0);
    ```

    Which of the following statements about this use of a class cast is true?

    A. The statement would compile and execute without error whether or not the cast is used.

    B. The statement would compile without error whether or not the cast is used, but the use of the cast prevents a runtime error when the first item in A is not a `String`.

    C. The statement would compile without error whether or not the cast is used, but there will be a runtime error if the first item in A is not a `String` whether or not the cast is used.

    D. The statement would cause a compile-time error if the cast were not used, and the use of the cast also prevents a runtime error if the first item in A is not a `String`.

    E. The statement would cause a compile-time error if the cast were not used, and there will be a runtime error if the first item in A is not a `String` even though the cast is used.

31. Consider implementing a hashtable to be used to store strings. Which of the following statements about the hash function is (are) true?

    I. If the hash function is called with strings A and B such that A is the same as B, then `hash(A)` must be the same as `hash(B)`.

    II. If the hash function is called with strings A and B such that A is not the same as B, then `hash(A)` must not be the same as `hash(B)`.

    III. If the hash function is called with strings A and B such that A comes before B in alphabetical order, then `hash(A)` must be less than `hash(B)`.

    A. I only

    B. II only

    C. I and II only

    D. I and III only

    E. I, II, and III

32. A min-heap is a good data structure to use to implement which of the following?

    A. A stack

    B. A queue

    C. A priority queue

    D. A singly linked list

    E. A doubly linked list

33. Assume that a subclass of the `LinkedList` class, called `SortedList`, has been defined, including the method specified below.

```
public void add(Comparable x) {
    // postcondition: adds x to the list in sorted order
    //                      (low to high)
    ...
}
```

Note that the `LinkedList` class has an `add` method with the same signature. Consider the following code segment:

```
LinkedList L1 = new LinkedList();
LinkedList L2 = new SortedList();
L1.add(new ArrayList());
L2.add(new Integer(5));
```

Which of the following statements about the two calls to `add` is true?

A. Both calls will call the `add` method of the `LinkedList` class, because both `L1` and `L2` are declared to be `LinkedLists`.

B. Both calls will call the `add` method of the `SortedList` class, because that method has overridden the `add` method of the `LinkedList` class.

C. Both calls will call the `add` method of the `LinkedList` class, because that is a standard java class, whereas `SortedList` is a user-defined class.

D. The first call will call the `add` method of the `LinkedList` class because `L1` points to a `LinkedList`, and the second call will call the `add` method of the `SortedList` class because `L2` points to a `SortedList`.

E. The first call will call the `add` method of the `LinkedList` class because the `ArrayList` argument is not a `Comparable` object, and the second call will call the `add` method of the `SortedList` class because the `Integer` argument is a `Comparable` object.

34. Consider designing classes to represent different kinds of animals: mammals, reptiles, birds, and insects. Which of the following is the best design?

A. Use five unrelated classes: `Animal`, `Mammal`, `Reptile`, `Bird`, and `Insect`.

B. Use one class, `Animal`, with four fields: `Mammal`, `Reptile`, `Bird`, and `Insect`.

C. Use one class, `Animal`, with four subclasses: `Mammal`, `Reptile`, `Bird`, and `Insect`.

D. Use five classes, `Animal`, `Mammal`, `Reptile`, `Bird`, and `Insect`, with `Mammal` as a subclass of `Animal`, `Reptile` as a subclass of `Mammal`, and so on.

E. Use four classes, `Mammal`, `Reptile`, `Bird`, and `Insect`, each with an `Animal` subclass.

Questions 35 and 36 rely on the following information:

Assume that circular linked lists are implemented using the standard `ListNode` class and that the `numNodes` method shown below has been added to the `ListNode` class. Method `numNodes` was intended to return the number of nodes in the circular linked list containing the node whose `numNodes` method was called. However, the method does not always work correctly. (Line numbers are included for reference.)

```
1. public int numNodes( ) {
2. // precondition:  this node is part of a circular linked list.
3.     Object tmp = value;
4.     int count = 1;
5.     ListNode L = next;
6.     while (!L.value.equals(tmp)) {
7.         count++;
8.         L = L.next;
9.     }
10.    return count;
11. }
```

35. Which of the following best characterizes the circular linked lists for which method `numNodes` does not work correctly?

    A. Circular linked lists with just one node

    B. Circular linked lists with more than one node

    C. Circular linked lists in which every node contains a different value

    D. Circular linked lists in which two nodes contain the same value

    E. Circular linked lists in which some node contains the same value as the node whose `numNodes` method was called

36. Which of the following changes fixes method `numNodes` so that it works correctly for every list that satisfies its precondition?

    A. Change line 3 to `ListNode tmp = this;`, remove line 5, change line 6 to `while (tmp != null)`, and replace line 8 with: `tmp = tmp.next;`.

    B. Change line 3 to `ListNode tmp = this;`, and change line 6 to `while (L != tmp)`.

    C. Change line 4 to `int count=0;`.

    D. Remove line 3, and change line 6 to `while (L != null)`.

    E. Change line 5 to `ListNode L = this;`.

37. Assume that variable L is a ListNode and has been initialized to point to the first node of a nonempty singly linked list. Which of the following code segments sets variable isOdd to true if there is an odd number of nodes in the list pointed to by L, and to false otherwise?

A.
```
isOdd = true;
while (L != null) {
    L = L.getNext();
    isOdd = !isOdd;
}
```

B.
```
isOdd = false;
while (L != null) {
    L = L.getNext();
    isOdd = !isOdd;
}
```

C.
```
isOdd = true;
while (L != null) {
    L = L.getNext();
    isOdd = isOdd || isOdd;
}
```

D.
```
isOdd = false;
while (L != null) {
    L = L.getNext();
    isOdd = isOdd || isOdd;
}
```

E.
```
isOdd = true;
while (L != null) {
    L = L.getNext();
    isOdd = isOdd && isOdd;
}
```

38. Assume that variables L, tmp, and `previous` are `ListNodes` with values as illustrated below.

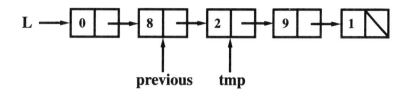

    Which of the following code segments removes the node pointed to by `tmp` from the list pointed to by L?

    A. `tmp = null;`

    B. `previous.setNext(tmp.getNext());`
       `tmp.setNext(null);`

    C. `tmp.setValue(previous.getValue());`

    D. `previous = tmp.getNext();`
       `tmp.setNext(null);`

    E. `tmp.setNext(previous);`

39. Assume that p and q are `String` variables and that the expression

    `(p != q)`

    evaluates to `true`. Which of the following must also evaluate to `true`?

    I. `!p.equals(q)`
    II. `p.length() != q.length()`
    III. `(p==null) || (q==null)`

    A. I only

    B. II only

    C. III only

    D. I and II

    E. None of the expressions necessarily evaluates to `true`.

40. Assume that T is a binary tree with N nodes (but is *not* a binary search tree). Which of the following operations cannot always be performed in O(N) time?

    A. Convert T to a binary search tree.

    B. Count the number of leaves in T.

    C. Find the smallest value in T.

    D. Add 1 to every value in T.

    E. Copy the values in T into an array of length N.

AB Practice Examination 2

Section II

Time — 1 hour and 45 minutes
Number of questions — 4
Percent of total grade — 50

Question 1

This question involves finding multiletter runs in a string. A *multiletter run* means the same letter twice or more in a row. For example, the string "aabcccde" has two multiletter runs: "aa" and "ccc".

Part (a)

Write method multiRunPosition, as started below. Method multiRunPosition should find the first multiletter run in string S, and it should return the position of the first letter in the run. If S does not contain any multiletter runs, multiRunPosition should return −1.

For example:

String S	Result of the call multiRunPosition(S)
"happy"	2
"aardvark"	0
"abbbcc"	1
"abc"	−1

Complete method `multiRunPosition` below.

```
public static int multiRunPosition( String S ) {
// precondition: S contains only lowercase letters
// postcondition: returns the position of the first letter of the
//                first multiletter run in S;
//                if there are no multiletter runs in S, returns -1
```

Part (b)

Write method `removeChar`, as started below. Method `removeChar` should return a string that is the same as its string parameter S, except that the character at position k has been removed. (Assume that, as specified by `removeChar`'s precondition, the value of k is in the range 0 to `S.length()` - 1.)

For example:

String S	Method call	Value returned by the call
`"abcde"`	`removeChar(S, 0)`	`"bcde"`
`"abcde"`	`removeChar(S, 1)`	`"acde"`
`"abcde"`	`removeChar(S, 2)`	`"abde"`
`"abcde"`	`removeChar(S, 3)`	`"abce"`
`"abcde"`	`removeChar(S, 4)`	`"abcd"`

Complete method `removeChar` below.

```
public static String removeChar( String S, int k ) {
// precondition:  0 <= k < S.length()
//                S is c_0 c_1 ... c_n
// postcondition: returns the string c_0 c_1 ... c_{k-1} c_{k+1} ... c_n
```

Part (c)

Write method removeRuns, as started below. Method removeRuns should return a string that is the same as its string parameter S except that all multiletter runs in S have been converted to single letters.

For example:

String S	Value returned by the call removeRuns (S)
"happy"	"hapy"
"aabccc"	"abc"
"aaabc"	"abc"
"abc"	"abc"

In writing removeRuns, you may include calls to methods multiRunPosition and removeChar, specified above in Parts (a) and (b). Assume that multiRunPosition and removeChar work as specified, regardless of what you wrote for Parts (a) and (b).

Complete method removeRuns below.

```
public static String removeRuns( String S ) {
// precondition: S contains only lowercase letters
```

Question 2

For many board games (e.g., chess, checkers, and go), the board can be represented using a two-dimensional array of integers, where the value in position [j][k] tells what piece (if any) is currently at that position. When deciding what move to make next, it is often useful to look for certain important patterns on the board.

These ideas lead to the following (partially specified) classes:

```
public class Position {
    /*** fields ***/
    private int row;
    private int column;

    /*** constructor ***/
    public Position(int theRow, int theCol) {
        row = theRow;
        col = theCol;
    }
}

public class BoardGame {
    /*** fields ***/
    private int[][] board;

    /*** public methods ***/
    public BoardGame() { ... }  // constructor
    public Position patternPos( int[][] pattern ) { ... }
    public Position rotatedPatternPos(int[][] pattern ) { ... }

    /*** private methods ***/
    private static int[][] rotate( int[][] A ) { ... }
}
```

Part (a)

Write the `patternPos` method of the `BoardGame` class, as started below. The `patternPos` method looks for the given pattern in the `board` array, and it returns the position in the `board` array where the upper-left corner of the pattern was found (if the pattern occurs more than once in the `board` array, the position corresponding to any of those occurances can be returned). If the pattern does not occur in the `board` array, method `patternPos` returns `null`.

For example, assume that the `board` array is as follows:

1	2	3	4
5	6	7	8
9	10	11	12

Below are the results of some calls to `patternPos`.

<table>
<tr><td align="center">pattern array</td><td align="center">Value returned by the call
patternPos(pattern)</td></tr>
</table>

1	2	3
5	6	7

(0,0)

6	7
10	11

(1,1)

12

(2,3)

6	2
7	3

null

1	3
5	7

null

Complete method `patternPos` below.

```
public Position patternPos( int[][] pattern ) {
// precondition: both board and pattern are nonempty, rectangular
//                arrays
// postcondition: if pattern occurs in the board array, returns
//                the position in the array where the upper-
//                left-hand corner of the pattern was found;
//                otherwise, returns null
```

Part (b)

Write the private `rotate` method of the `BoardGame` class, as started below. The `rotate` method returns a rectangular, two-dimensional array that contains the same values as its parameter A, but rotated 90 degrees clockwise. (The `BoardGame`'s `rotate` method can be used to rotate a given pattern so that it can be found in different orientations on the board.)

Below are some examples of calls to `rotate`.

<table>
<tr><td colspan="5" align="center">Array A</td><td></td><td colspan="3" align="center">Value returned by the call
rotate(A)</td></tr>
</table>

Array A:

1	2	3
6	7	8

Value returned by the call rotate(A):

6	1
7	2
8	3

Array A:

1	2	3	4	5
6	7	8	9	10

Value returned:

6	1
7	2
8	3
9	4
10	5

Array A:

1	2	3	4	5
6	7	8	9	10
11	12	13	14	15

Value returned:

11	6	1
12	7	2
13	8	3
14	9	4
15	10	5

Note that when array A is rotated, row 0 becomes the last column; row 1 becomes the second-to-last column, and so on.

Complete method `rotate` below.

```
private static int[][] rotate( int[][] A ) {
// precondition: A is a nonempty, rectangular array
```

Part (c)

Write the rotatedPatternPos method of the BoardGame class, as started below. The rotatedPatternPos method looks in the board array for the given pattern rotated 90, 180, or 270 degrees clockwise. It returns the position in the board array where the upper-left corner of the rotated pattern was found. If the rotated pattern occurs more than once in the board array, the position corresponding to any of those occurances can be returned. If the rotated pattern does not occur in the board array, method rotatedPatternPos returns null.

For example, assume that the board array is as follows:

1	2	3	4
5	6	7	8
9	10	11	12

Below are the results of some calls to rotatedPatternPos.

pattern array	Value returned by the call rotatedPatternPos (pattern)	Degrees of rotation
3 7 2 6	(0,1)	90
7 6 3 2	(0,1)	180
6 2 7 3	(0,1)	270
4 8 12 3 7 11	(0,2)	90

In writing rotatedPatternPos, you may include calls to methods patternPos and rotate, specified above in Parts (a) and (b). Assume that those methods work as specified, regardless of what you wrote for Parts (a) and (b).

Complete method `rotatedPatternPos` below.

```
public Position rotatedPatternPos( int[][] pattern ) {
// precondition: both board and pattern are nonempty, rectangular
//               arrays
// postcondition: if pattern occurs in the board array rotated 90,
//                180, or 270 degrees clockwise, then returns the
//                position in the array where the upper-left-hand
//                corner of the pattern was found;
//                otherwise, returns null
```

Question 3

Assume that the Name class, which is partially defined below, is used to represent people's first names.

```
public class Name {
    /*** fields ***/
    private String myName;

    /*** methods ***/
    public Name( String S ) { myName = S; }  // constructor
    public int length() { return myName.length(); }
    public String prefix( int k ) { ... }
    public String suffix( int k ) { ... }
    public boolean isNickname( Name n ) { ... }
}
```

Part (a)

Write the `prefix` method of the Name class, as started below. The `prefix` method should return a string containing the first k characters in the name. If the name has fewer than k characters, the `prefix` method should return the entire string.

For example, assume that name N represents the name "Sandy". Below are some examples of calls to N's `prefix` method.

k	Result of the call N.prefix(k)
0	""
1	"S"
2	"Sa"
3	"San"
5	"Sandy"
6	"Sandy"

Complete method `prefix` below.

```
public String prefix( int k ) {
// precondition: k >= 0
// postcondition: returns a string containing the first k letters
//                in this name; if this name has fewer than k
//                letters, returns the whole name
```

Part (b)

Write the `suffix` method of the `Name` class, as started below. The `suffix` method should return a string containing the last k characters in the name. If the name has fewer than k characters, the `suffix` method should return the entire string.

For example, assume that name N represents the name "Sandy". Below are some examples of calls to N's `suffix` method.

k	Result of the call N.`suffix( k )`
0	""
1	"y"
2	"dy"
3	"ndy"
5	"Sandy"
6	"Sandy"

Complete method `suffix` below.

```
public String suffix( int k ) {
// precondition: k >= 0
// postcondition: returns a string containing the last k letters in
//                this name; if this name has fewer than k letters,
//                returns the whole name
```

Part (c)

Write the `isNickname` method of the `Name` class, as started below. The `isNickname` method should return `true` if and only if its parameter `nick` is made up of two parts:

1. A nonempty string that is a prefix of this name
2. The suffix `"ie"`

Below are some examples.

Name represented by N	Name represented by nick	Value returned by the call N.isNickname(nick)
Susan	Susie	true
David	Davie	true
Ann	Annie	true
Susan	Sus	false
Ann	Robbie	false
David	Davy	false

In writing method `isNickname`, you may include calls to methods `prefix` and `suffix`, specified above in Parts (a) and (b). Assume that both methods work as specified, regardless of what you wrote in Parts (a) and (b).

Complete method `isNickname` below.

```
public boolean isNickname( Name nick ) {
// precondition: nick is not null
```

Question 4

Assume that binary trees are implemented using the standard `TreeNode` class. For this question, you will augment the `TreeNode` class by adding the following three methods:

```
public Object rightmostLeafVal( )
// postcondition: returns the value stored in the rightmost leaf of
//                the tree rooted at this node

public Object pushLeavesRight( Object inval )
// precondition: the leaves of the tree rooted at this node contain
//               values v1, v2, ..., vn
// postcondition: the leaves of the tree rooted at this node contain
//                values inval, v1, v2, ..., vn-1;
//                returns value vn

public void rotateLeaves( )
// precondition: the leaves of the tree rooted at this node contain
//               values v1, v2, ..., vn
// postcondition: the leaves of the tree rooted at this node contain
//                values vn, v1, v2, ..., vn-1
```

Part (a)

Write the `rightmostLeafVal` method of the `TreeNode` class. Method `rightmostLeafVal` should return the value stored in the rightmost leaf of the tree rooted at the node whose `rightmostLeafVal` method is called.

For example:

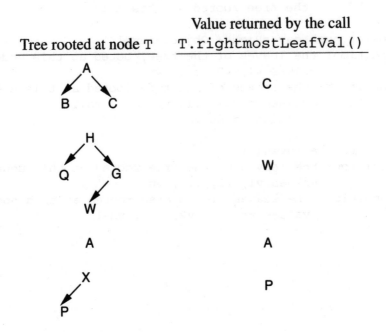

Tree rooted at node T	Value returned by the call `T.rightmostLeafVal()`
	C
	W
	A
	P

Complete method `rightmostLeafVal` below.

```
public Object rightmostLeafVal( ) {
// postcondition: returns the value stored in the rightmost leaf
//                of the tree rooted at this node
```

Part (b)

Write the `pushLeavesRight` method of the `TreeNode` class. Method `pushLeavesRight` should change the values in all of the leaves of the tree rooted at the node whose `pushLeavesRight` method is called, inserting the value `inval` into the leftmost leaf, inserting the value that was originally in the leftmost leaf into the second-to-leftmost leaf, and so on, finally returning the value that was in the rightmost leaf. For example:

Initial tree rooted at node T	The tree after the call T.pushLeavesRight("X")	Value returned by the call

Complete method `pushLeavesRight` below.

```
public Object pushLeavesRight( Object inval ) {
// precondition: the leaves of the tree rooted at this node contain
//               values v1, v2, ..., vn
// postcondition: the leaves of the tree rooted at this node contain
//               values inval, v1, v2, ..., vn-1;
//               returns value vn
```

Part (c)

Write the `rotateLeaves` method of the `TreeNode` class. Method `rotateLeaves` should change the values in all of the leaves of the tree rooted at the node whose `rotateLeaves` method was called, inserting `Object vn` from the rightmost leaf of the tree into the leftmost leaf, inserting the value that was originally in the leftmost leaf into the second-to-leftmost leaf, and so on.

For example:

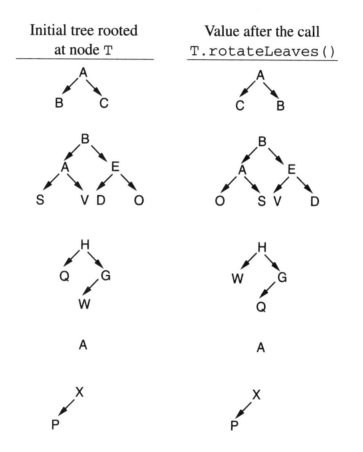

In writing method `rotateLeaves`, you may include calls to methods `rightmostLeafVal` and `pushLeavesRight`, specified above in Parts (a) and (b). Assume that both methods work as specified, regardless of what you wrote for Parts (a) and (b).

Complete method `rotateLeaves` below.

```
public void rotateLeaves( ) {
// precondition: the leaves of the tree rooted at this node contain
//                values v1, v2, ..., vn
// postcondition: the leaves of the tree rooted at this node contain
//                values vn, v1, v2, ..., vn-1
```

Answers to AB Practice Examination 2

Section I

1.	C	21.	C
2.	A	22.	C
3.	E	23.	C
4.	A	24.	A
5.	B	25.	C
6.	D	26.	D
7.	E	27.	A
8.	C	28.	A
9.	C	29.	B
10.	A	30.	E
11.	D	31.	A
12.	C	32.	C
13.	B	33.	D
14.	E	34.	C
15.	C	35.	E
16.	D	36.	B
17.	D	37.	B
18.	B	38.	B
19.	D	39.	E
20.	C	40.	A

Answers to AB Practice Examination 2

Section II

Question 1

Part (a)

Version 1

Compare each character in S with the next character.

```
public static int multiRunPosition( String S ) {
// precondition: S contains only lowercase letters
// postcondition: returns the position of the first letter of the
//                first multiletter run in S;
//                if there are no multiletter runs in S, returns -1
    for (int k=0; k<S.length()-1; k++) {
        if (S.substring(k, k+1).equals(S.substring(k+1, k+2)))
            return k;
    }
    return -1;
}
```

Version 2

Compare each character in S with the previous character; be sure to return the position of the previous character when a match is found.

```
public static int multiRunPosition( String S ) {
// precondition: S contains only lowercase letters
// postcondition: returns the position of the first letter of the
//                first multiletter run in S;
//                if there are no multiletter runs in S, returns -1
    for (int k=1; k<S.length(); k++) {
        if (S.substring(k-1, k).equals(S.substring(k, k+1)))
            return k-1;
    }
    return -1;
}
```

Part (b)

Version 1

Concatenate two substrings.

```
public static String removeChar( String S, int k ) {
    // precondition: 0 <= k < S.length()
    return( S.substring(0, k) + S.substring(k+1) );
}
```

Version 2

Concatenate individual characters.

```
public static String removeChar( String S, int k ) {
    // precondition: 0 <= k < S.length()
    String newS = "";
    for (int j=0; j<S.length(); j++) {
        if (j != k) newS += S.substring(j, j+1);
    }
    return newS;
}
```

Part (c)

Version 1

Remove one letter at a time.

```
public static String removeRuns( String S ) {
    // precondition: S contains only lowercase letters
    String newS = S;
    int k = multiRunPosition(newS);
    while (k != -1) {
        newS = removeChar(newS, k);
        k = multiRunPosition(newS);
    }
    return newS;
}
```

Version 2

Remove all letters after the first in each multiletter run.

```
public static String removeRuns( String S ) {
    // precondition: S contains only lowercase letters
    String newS = S;
    int k = multiRunPosition(newS);
    while (k != -1) {
        // remove all but the first letter in the run
        String oneLetter = newS.substring(k, k+1);
        int j = k+1;
        while (j<newS.length() &&
                newS.substring(j, j+1).equals(oneLetter)){
            newS = removeChar(newS, k);
        }
        k = multiRunPosition(newS);
    }
    return newS;
}
```

Common errors:

- Off-by-one errors (e.g., removing the wrong character)
- Using S instead of newS in some places (e.g., in the call to multiRunPosition)
- For Version 2, forgetting to test for j past the end of the string (so the expression newS.substring(j, j+1) causes an exception)

Question 2.

Part (a)

Note that method `patternPos` is much easier to write if you first write an auxiliary method that tests one position of the array to see whether there is a match using that position as the upper-left corner.

```
private boolean patternPosAux( int[][] pattern, int row, int col ) {
// precondition: pattern is a rectangular array;
//                row < pattern.length;
//                col < pattern[0].length
//                row + pattern.length-1 < board.length
// postcondition: returns true if pattern occurs in board with its
//                 upper-left corner at board[row][col];
//                 otherwise, returns false
    int patRow = 0, patCol;
    int boardRow = row, boardCol = col;
     while (patRow < pattern.length && boardRow < board.length) {
        patCol = 0;
        boardCol = col;
        while (patCol < pattern[0].length &&
               boardCol < board[0].length) {
           if (board[boardRow][boardCol] !=
               pattern[patRow][patCol]) {
               return false;
           }
           patCol++;
           boardCol++;
        }
        patRow++;
        boardRow++;
    }
    return true;
}

public Position patternPos( int[][] pattern ) {
// precondition: both board and pattern are nonempty, rectangular
//                arrays
// postcondition: if pattern occurs in the board array, returns
//                 the position in the array where the upper-left-hand
//                 corner of the pattern was found;
//                 otherwise, returns null
    for (int j=0; j<=board.length-pattern.length; j++) {
        for (int k=0; k<=board[0].length-pattern[0].length; k++) {
            if (patternPosAux(pattern, j, k)) {
                return new Position(j, k);
            }
        }
    }
    return null;
}
```

Common errors:

- Code that can cause index-out-of-bounds errors
- Forgetting to return the position where the pattern is found, or incorrect construction of that position

Part (b)

```
private static int[][] rotate( int[][] A ) {
// precondition: A is a nonempty, rectangular array
    int[][] newA = new int[A[0].length][A.length];
    int newrow, newcol = A.length-1;
     for (int j=0; j<A.length; j++) {
        newrow = 0;
        for (int k=0; k<A[0].length; k++) {
            newA[newrow][newcol] = A[j][k];
            newrow++;
        }
        newcol--;
    }
    return newA;
}
```

Common errors:

- Forgetting to allocate the new array, or allocating an array of the wrong size
- Copying the wrong values into the new array
- Forgetting to return the new array

Part (c)

Version 1

Use a loop to try each rotation in turn.

```
public Position rotatedPatternPos( int[][] pattern ) {
// precondition: both board and pattern are nonempty, rectangular
//                arrays
// postcondition: if pattern occurs in the board array rotated 90,
//                180, or 270 degrees clockwise, then returns the
//                position in the array where the upper-left-hand
//                corner of the pattern was found;
//                otherwise, returns null
    int[][] tmp = rotate(pattern);
    int rotation = 90;
    while (rotation <= 270) {
        Position p = patternPos(tmp);
        if (p != null) return p;
        rotation +=90;
        tmp = rotate(tmp);
    }
    return null;
}
```

Version 2

Try each rotation explicitly.

```
public Position rotatedPatternPos1( int[][] pattern ) {
// precondition: both board and pattern are nonempty, rectangular
//                arrays
// postcondition: if pattern occurs in the board array rotated 90,
//                180, or 270 degrees clockwise, then returns the
//                position in the array where the upper-left-hand
//                corner of the pattern was found;
//                otherwise, returns null
    int[][] tmp = rotate(pattern);
    Position p = patternPos(tmp);
    if (p != null) return p;
    tmp = rotate(tmp);
    p = patternPos(tmp);
    if (p != null) return p;
    tmp = rotate(tmp);
    p = patternPos(tmp);
    if (p != null) return p;
    return null;
}
```

Question 3

Part (a)

```
public String prefix( int k ) {
// precondition: k >= 0
// postcondition: returns a string containing the first k letters
//                in this name;
//                if this name has fewer than k letters,
//                returns the whole name
    if (myName.length() < k) return myName;
    else return myName.substring(0,k);
}
```

Common errors:

- Forgetting to check whether this name has fewer than k characters (or handling that case incorrectly)

- Incorrect call to myName.substring

Part (b)

```
public String suffix( int k ) {
// precondition: k >= 0
// postcondition: returns a string containing the last k letters in
//                this name; if this name has fewer than k letters,
//                returns the whole name
    int from;
    if (k > myName.length()) from = 0;
    else from = myName.length() - k;
    return myName.substring(from);
}
```

Part (c)

```
public boolean isNickname( Name n ) {
    if (!n.suffix(2).equals("ie")) return false;
    String pre1 = prefix(n.length() - 2);
    String pre2 = n.prefix(n.length() - 2);
    if (!pre1.equals(pre2)) return false;
    return true;
}
```

Question 4

Part (a)

Version 1

Use recursion.

```
public Object rightmostLeafVal( ) {
// postcondition: returns the value stored in the rightmost leaf
//                of the tree rooted at this node
    if (left == null && right == null) {
        // this node is a leaf--return its value
        return value;
    }
    else if (right == null) return left.rightmostLeafVal();
    else return right.rightmostLeafVal();
}
```

Common error:

- Returning the value at the current node whenever its right subtree is empty (instead of only when the current node is a leaf)

Version 2

Use iteration.

```
public Object rightmostLeafVal1( ) {
// postcondition: returns the value stored in the rightmost leaf
//                of the tree rooted at this node
    TreeNode n = this;
    while (true) {
        if (n.left == null && n.right == null) {
            // n is rightmost leaf -- return its value
            return n.value;
        }
        if (n.right != null) n = n.right;
        else n = n.left;
    }
}
```

Part (b)

```
public Object pushLeavesRight( Object inval ) {
// precondition: the leaves of the tree rooted at this node contain
//                values v1, v2, ..., vn
// postcondition: the leaves of the tree rooted at this node contain
//                values inval, v1, v2, ..., vn-1;
//                returns value vn
    if (left == null && right == null) {
        // at a leaf--change its value, returning the original
        // value
        Object tmp = value;
        value = inval;
        return tmp;
    }
    // here if not at a leaf
    if (left != null) {
        inval = left.pushLeavesRight(inval);
        if (right != null) return right.pushLeavesRight(inval);
        else return inval;
    }
    else return right.pushLeavesRight(inval);
}
```

Part (c)

```
public void rotateLeaves( ) {
// precondition: the leaves of the tree rooted at this node contain
//                values v1, v2, ..., vn
// postcondition: the leaves of the tree rooted at this node contain
//                values vn, v1, v2, ..., vn-1
    pushLeavesRight(rightmostLeafVal());
}
```

Glossary

actual parameter: One of the values passed when a method is called (see also "formal parameter").

add: One of the operations for many of the AP CS standard classes and interfaces, including `ArrayList` and `LinkedList`.

argument: Same as "actual parameter."

arithmetic operators: `+ - * / %` (addition, subtraction, multiplication, division, and modulus).

assignment operators: `= += -= *= /= %=` (plain assignment, add-then-assign, subtract-then-assign, multiply-then-assign, divide-then-assign, and modulus-then-assign).

average case time/space (AB only): The amount of time or space that an algorithm or data structure will require on average.

base case: Every recursive method must have a base case, which is a condition under which the method does not call itself.

big-O (AB only): Notation for expressing the time or space required by an algorithm.

binary search: An efficient technique for finding a value in a sorted array; a value can be found in an array of N elements in time proportional to $log_2 N$ (see also "sequential search").

binary search tree (AB only): A data structure that supports efficient insertion and look-up of ordered values ($O(\log N)$ if the tree is balanced).

binary tree: A tree in which every node has at most two children.

casting: Used to convert one datatype to another. For example: `int(3.5)` converts the floating-point value 3.5 to an integer (by truncating it to 3).

circular linked list (AB only): A linked list in which the last node points back to the first node.

class: The basic mechanism provided by object-oriented languages to support abstract data types.

compound assignment: `+= -= *= /= %=` (add-then-assign, subtract-then-assign, multiply-then-assign, divide-then-assign, and modulus-then-assign).

constant time/space (AB only): The amount of time or space required by an algorithm or data structure is independent of the amount of data; if the amount of data doubles, the amount of time or space will stay the same.

constructor: A class's constructor(s) should initialize the fields of the class.

decrement operator: `--` (subtracts one from its operand).

default constructor: A constructor with no arguments.

dequeue (AB only): One of the standard queue operations; it removes and returns the item at the front of the queue.

doubly linked list (AB only): A linked list in which each node has two pointers: one that points to the next node in the list and one that points to the previous node in the list (see also "singly linked list," "circular linked list").

dynamic dispatch: The technique used to determine which version of a method that has been overridden by a subclass is actually called at runtime.

efficiency: How much time and/or space is required by an algorithm or data structure.

enqueue (AB only): One of the standard queue operations; it adds a given item to the end of the queue.

equality operators: `==` and `!=` (equal to and not equal to).

exponential time/space (AB only): If the amount of data increases by one, the amount of time or space required by the algorithm or data structure will double.

field (nonstatic): A variable associated with each instance of a class (see also "instance variable").

field (static): A variable associated with a class (see also "instance variable").

for-loop: A loop of the form `for` (*init-expression*; *test-expression*; *update-expression*) *statement*.

formal parameter: One of the identifiers listed in a method header that corresponds to the values passed when the method is called (see also "actual parameter").

hash function (AB only): A function that maps values to integers; used to determine where to store a value in a hashtable.

hashtable (AB only): A data structure used to support efficient insert and look-up operations (can have O(1) average-case time).

heap (AB only): A data structure that can be used to provide an efficient implementation of a priority queue.

if statement: A statement of the form `if` (*expression*) *statement* or `if` (*expression*) *statement* `else` *statement*.

increment operator: `++` (adds one to its operand).

inorder traversal (AB only): Visiting all nodes of a binary tree using the following algorithm: visit the left subtree in inorder, visit the root, and visit the right subtree in inorder.

insertion sort: A sorting algorithm that takes time proportional to N^2 to sort N items.

instance variable: Another name for a field of a class.

isEmpty (AB only): One of the standard stack, queue, and priority queue operations; it returns `true` if the stack, queue, or priority queue is empty, and otherwise it returns `false`.

iteration: One execution of the body of a loop.

iterator (AB only): One of the AP CS standard Java interfaces; it provides a way to iterate through the objects in some collection of objects, one at a time.

length: For a one-dimensional array A, `A.length` is the length of the array; for a rectangular two-dimensional array A, `A.length` is the number of rows in the array, and `A[0].length` is the number of columns in the array. For a `String S`, `S.length()` is the number of characters in the string.

linear time/space (AB only): If the amount of data doubles, the amount of time or space required by the algorithm or data structure will also double.

linked list (AB only): A common data structure used to represent an ordered collection of objects (see also "circular linked list," "doubly linked list," "singly linked list").

ListNode (AB only): The standard AP CS class used to implement the nodes of a linked list.

logarithmic time/space (AB only): If the amount of data doubles, the amount of time or space required by the algorithm or data structure will increase by one.

logical operators: `!` `&&` `||` (logical NOT, logical AND, and logical OR).

merge sort: A sorting algorithm that takes time proportional to $log_2 N$ to sort N items.

min-heap (AB only): See "heap."

new operator: Used to create a new instance of an `Object` (it allocates memory from free storage).

null: A special value used for a pointer that does not point to any memory location.

overloading: Defining two versions of a method in the same class with the same name but with different numbers or types of parameters.

overriding: Defining a method in a subclass with the same name and the same numbers and types of parameters as a method in a superclass. Dynamic dispatch is used to determine which version is actually called at runtime.

parameter: Same as "formal parameter."

peekFront (AB only): One of the standard queue operations; it returns the item at the front of the queue without removing it.

peekMin (AB only): One of the standard priority queue operations; it returns the smallest item from the priority queue without removing it.

peekTop (AB only): One of the standard stack operations; it returns the item at the top of the stack without removing it.

pointer: A location whose value is another location (a memory address). The computer memory associated with an `Object` holds a pointer to the actual object.

pointer equality: When two pointers are compared using `==` or `!=`, they are considered equal only if they point to the same address; if they point to different addresses that contain the same value, the pointers are considered not equal. Pointer equality is also the default for an object's `equals` method.

pointer parameters: Objects are really pointers, so when an object is passed as a value parameter, although the object itself cannot be changed by the method, the contents of the location that it points to can be changed.

pop (AB only): One of the standard stack operations; it removes and returns the top item.

postcondition: A method's postcondition specifies what will be true when the method returns, assuming that the method's preconditions are satisfied when it is called.

postorder traversal (AB only): Visiting all nodes of a binary tree using the following algorithm: visit the left subtree in postorder, visit the right subtree in postorder, and visit the root.

precondition: A method's precondition specifies what is expected to be true whenever the method is called.

preorder traversal (AB only): Visiting all nodes of a binary tree using the following algorithm: visit the root, visit the left subtree in preorder, and visit the right subtree in preorder.

priority queue (AB only): A data structure used to store objects with an underlying ordering (i.e., objects that could be sorted). Priority queue operations include inserting an object and removing (and returning) the smallest object currently in the priority queue.

private: One of the levels of access that can be specified for a class's fields and methods; private fields and methods can only be accessed/called by an instance of the class (see also "public").

public: One of the levels of access that can be specified for a class's fields and methods; public fields and methods can be accessed/called by a client of the class (see also "private").

push (AB only): One of the standard stack operations; it adds a given item to the top of the stack.

quadratic time/space: (AB only): If the amount of data doubles, the amount of time or space required by the algorithm or data structure will quadruple.

queue (AB only): A first-in-first-out data structure.

quick sort: A sorting algorithm that takes time proportional to $log_2 N$ to sort N items if good choices are made for the pivot items, and otherwise can take time proportional to N^2.

recursive method: A method that calls itself (either directly or indirectly).

relational operators: < <= > >= (less than, less than or equal to, greater than, and greater than or equal to).

removeMin (AB only): One of the standard priority queue operations; it removes and returns the smallest item from the priority queue.

return statement: Executing a `return` statement causes control to be transferred from the currently executing method to the calling method; for a non-`void` method, a `return` statement is also used to return a value.

return type: The type returned by a non-`void` method.

selection sort: A sorting algorithm that takes time proportional to N^2 to sort N items.

sequential search: An algorithm that looks for a value in an array by starting with the first element and examining each element in turn; it requires time proportional to the size of the array on average (see also "binary search").

short-circuit evaluation: Expressions involving the logical AND and OR operators are guaranteed to be evaluated from left to right, and evaluation stops as soon as the final value is known.

singly linked list (AB only): A linked list in which each node has only one pointer, which points to the next node in the list (see also "doubly linked list," "circular linked list").

subclass: A class that extends an existing class. (The subclass should have an "*is-a*" relationship with the class that it extends.)

superclass: A class that is extended by a new class.

stack (AB only): A first-in-last-out data structure.

static: A field or method of a class associated with the class itself rather than with an instance of the class.

String: A standard Java class used to represent strings (sequences of characters).

traversal (AB only): An algorithm for visiting all nodes of a binary tree (see also "inorder traversal," "postorder traversal," "preorder traversal").

tree height (AB only): The height of an empty tree is 0; the height of a nonempty tree is the number of nodes in the longest path from the root to a leaf.

tree leaf (AB only): A tree node with no outgoing edges.

TreeNode (AB only): The standard AP CS class used to implement the nodes of a tree.

tree parent (AB only): If a tree includes an edge from node n to node m, then n is the parent of m.

tree root (AB only): A tree node with no incoming edges (no parent).

value parameter: In Java, all parameters are passed by value: when a method is called, the actual parameters are copied into new locations (named with the names of the formal parameters); therefore, changes made to the formal parameter by the called method do not change the corresponding actual parameter.

void: The type of a method that performs an action rather than computing (and returning) a result.

while-loop: A loop of the form while (*expression*) *statement*. A while-loop may execute zero times (see also "for-loop").

worst-case time/space (AB only): The amount of time or space that an algorithm or data structure will require in the worst case.

Index